Rough Sex

This book is for the women who appear in it.
It is also for everyone else who struggles under the tyranny of patriarchy.

Rough Sex

Sexual Practice and the Limits of Consent

Alexandra Fanghanel

EDINBURGH
University Press

Edinburgh University Press is one of the leading university presses in the UK. Publishing new research in the arts and humanities, EUP connects people and ideas to inspire creative thinking, open new perspectives and shape the world we live in. For more information, visit www.edinburghuniversitypress.com.

Edinburgh University Press Ltd
13 Infirmary Street, Edinburgh EH1 1LT

Typeset in 10.5/14 New Caledonia LT Std by
Cheshire Typesetting Ltd, Cuddington, Cheshire
Printed and bound in the UK using 100% renewable electricity by
CPI Group (UK) Ltd

A CIP record for this book is available from the British Library

ISBN 978 1 3995 4157 2 (hardback)
ISBN 978 1 3995 4159 6 (webready PDF)
ISBN 978 1 3995 4160 2 (epub)

EU Authorised Representative:
Easy Access System Europe
Mustamäe tee 50, 10621 Tallinn, Estonia
gpsr.requests@easproject.com

MIX
Paper | Supporting responsible forestry
FSC
www.fsc.org
FSC® C013604

This book is printed using paper from well-managed forests, recycling and other controlled sources

Contents

Acknowledgements

This book was not easy to write. The struggle with the subject matter, the implications of the arguments that I wanted to make, and the usual writerly wanderings through self-doubt and anguish mean that I have spent far too long on it and have dragged it around the company of far too many people who have each, in their way, helped me along.

Of course, I am indebted to the forbearance of my splendid colleagues at the University of Greenwich School of Law and Criminology, who make work a pleasure and whom I am humbled to know and to sing karaoke with. Especially the hardcore brilliance of the erstwhile Gender, Deviance and Society research group who have been great fun to work with. I was also fortunate to receive funding from the University of Greenwich to support the acquisition of transcripts as well as the acquisition of (some) time to write about them.

My mates and colleagues Dr Emma Milne and Dr Lousie Hewitt both helped me to understand what it was that I was supposed to be doing, methodologically, with this project and I could not have got started without them. Thanks, too, to Professor Gayle Letherby for helpful comments on the text and for my colleagues in the Community-Academic Consortium for Research on Alternative Sexualities who have championed this work.

Thanks are also due to the court clerks around the country who helped me to find transcripts and ask for the right material, and who facilitated access to the data that you read here.

My best gals Natasha Dhumma and Ruth Jacob are STILL the baddest babes. Their amazingness is out of this world. Not enough people know this about them, so I am just laying that fact out here.

The writing of this book would not have been possible without the stalwart support of Ludovic Coupaye, whose anthropological eyes have read, critiqued and challenged my ideas for the past fifteen years and whose enormous heart has tended to my needs and those of our exuberant children throughout the writing of this book.

Thanks too, to Danger, who keeps me vital.

Read This First

This book details aspects of what happens in criminal cases in which women have been killed or injured by men during sexual encounters which, we are told, both parties consented to. I have used court transcripts to examine these as examples of rough sex which has gone awry. In order to analyse these cases, I have used language from court transcripts, and I have outlined the facts of the cases. The language of the cases is often bald and crude. The acts that have taken place are described in explicit ways. Many of these make for bleak reading, and it can be upsetting to spend time with subject matter that is so violent, however that violence expresses itself.

Before embarking on this book as a reader, I urge you to be mindful of the fact that the content of the cases might make for tough reading. Do what you need to do to make it work for you.

1. Spectacular Sexuality and its Troubles

> On your account, after beating her, Natalie's requests became more extreme. She asked you to insert a bottle of spray carpet cleaner into her vagina, as a sexual stimulant. This was a large object with a trigger. It became lodged in her vagina, and you could not get it out. You went to get a bottle of lubricant to try and remove it. The pathological evidence was that the bottle caused lacerations to her vagina resulting in arterial and venous haemorrhage … It seems to me, [that this] was something which came about, on your account, because once you had beaten Natalie, she wanted something more extreme done to her. As I have said, I am prepared to accept in your favour that she instigated this. (Sentencing remarks in the case of *R* v. *Broadhurst*, 2018)

In 2018, John Broadhurst pleaded guilty to the manslaughter of his partner, Natalie Connolly, following a night of considerable alcohol consumption and 'extreme' sexual practices. He was sentenced to three years and eight months in prison. One of the reasons his sentence was so short was that, in mitigation, Broadhurst claimed that what took place between himself and his partner occurred 'within the boundaries of her masochistic desires'. That is, *with her consent*.

In 2018, at the time that media scrutiny of this case was gaining momentum, I was working on a project that analysed the role that consent plays in sexual encounters known as bondage and sadomasochism (BDSM), or what might, in some contexts, be called 'rough sex' or 'extreme' sex practice. I was immersed in BDSM culture: attending events, observing practice, interviewing practitioners and examining what happens when a subculture interacts with the mainstream: when these two worlds collide (Fanghanel, 2019; 2020). It is against this background that I became aware of the *Broadhurst* case, the facts of which seemed to shed light on this precise dynamic: what happens when subcultures interact with the mainstream of the judicial system? What occurs at this point of connection? What does this mean for sexual justice? I was incredulous about the stated facts and outcome of the case. How did they know that the injuries which were, in part, responsible for her death, were caused with Connolly's consent? How could they tell that her consent was meaningful? Or rather, I was not incredulous that this happened – men's violence against women is not surprising – rather, I was incredulous that the courts were so credulous. So ready to simply take his word for it.

Scholars of sexual subcultures will be aware that much of what constitutes BDSM practice is criminalised across the global north (Khan, 2020; Ridinger, 2006). In England and Wales, the case of *R* v. *Brown*, in which a group of men engaged in BDSM acts to which they had all consented confirms that there is no defence of consent to injury that is more than merely 'transient or trifling' (*R* V. *Donovan* [1934]1 2 KB 498, 509). In the USA, a similar principle that consent is not a defence in cases where people are injured as part of a BDSM encounter holds. The USA's Model Penal Code provides that a defence of consent to injury during sex might only be raised in cases where the injury is 'not serious'. In some US states, BDSM is criminalised, in others, the question is not yet settled. Similarly, in Canada, consent to sexual assault is not possible in cases where pain is inflicted on one or all of the parties (Khan, 2016b). The landscape is similar in much (though not all) of Europe.

The *Broadhurst* case is provocative, not only for the relatively short sentence that Broadhurst received, but also for the way that consent to sexual violence influenced the judge's comments in sentencing. This case managed to garner action around how consent is used in these instances. The campaign group We Can't Consent to This (WCCTT) was established in part in response to the *Broadhurst* case. Its principal focus was on eliminating the use of what became known as the 'consent defence' in circumstances where women are killed or injured during a sexual encounter (Mackenzie, 2023). Political and academic commentary also started to focus on how this argument was used to reduce a charge of murder to manslaughter, to reduce one of manslaughter to accidental death, and to mitigate sentencing when perpetrators *are* found guilty (Garnier & Harman, 2019; Edwards, 2015; Yardley, 2021; Bows & Herring, 2020).

Marc Garnier and Harriet Harman (2019), amongst others, argue that this so-called 'consent defence' is a revision of the 'she asked for it', victim-blaming maxim. Indeed, the work that WCCTT has achieved demonstrates that far from being unusual, claims that there was consent during a sexual encounter which employs violent themes are increasingly prevalent in cases coming to court. The first reported case where this claim appears was in 1972. Over the past two decades, the number of cases where a similar argument has been raised have proliferated. Since that year, a total of sixty-two cases where a woman has died during a sexual encounter have mobilised this consent claim, of which thirty-two were in the last ten years, and seventeen in the last five (Mackenzie, 2023, p. 153). Whether this increase is because BDSM and BDSM-adjacent practices have become more mainstream and so more practised, or whether it is simply because violence against women in sexual encounters has become more common, or because there appears to be a growing tolerance of the possibility of consent as mitigation, what this does tell us is that *something like the idea of a consent defence* appears to be emerging as a possibility within the socio-legal landscape.

As a result of campaigning around this issue, the Domestic Abuse Act 2021 was passed in England and Wales to introduce the offences of non-fatal strangulation and non-fatal suffocation. This confirmed that a consent defence could not apply to suffocation or strangulation if serious harm is caused to the person strangled and the dominant party intended to, or was reckless as to whether they would, cause serious harm to that person. The Act also enshrined in statute law the legal position established in *Brown*: that consent is no defence to serious harm caused for sexual gratification. Of course, in the Broadhurst case which provoked this response, it was not strangulation or suffocation which killed Connolly. As Emily Bradley (2023, p. 171) notes, these amendments will not inherently protect women killed or injured in this way. Indeed, lenient sentences are still passed in cases where men have killed women during a consensual sexual encounter despite the passing of this Act (see *R* v. *Pybus*, 2021). We are in murky terrain, and it looks like we are staying there, for now.

AN IMPASSE

Though it is true that BDSM clubs are not usually raided by the police and that people are mostly not arrested for participating in BDSM in their own homes, the fact remains that in many jurisdictions, much of what could be described as BDSM is criminalisable.[1] A number of scholars posit that a consent defence should be extended to BDSM sexual practice and that to withhold access to one has the effect of curtailing BDSM practitioners' liberty rights, including the right to establishing an 'enduring intimate relationship' (Haley, 2015, p. 631). They argue that moral distaste for BDSM – a

[1] Though it should be noted that licensing laws are used to shut down BDSM clubs and fetish nights (Spanner People, 1995; Khan, 2014; Doherty, 2022) which also has implications for how this subculture is figured in socio-legal contexts.

practice that has been called in court 'cruel' and 'uncivilised' (*R* v. *Brown*, 1993, p. 9) – is not enough of a justification for its continued criminalisation (Haley, 2015, p. 645; Khan, 2016a). For these activists, the criminalisation of BDSM activities is akin to the criminalisation of male homosexual encounters in the last century (Haley, 2015, p. 631). Indeed, as Ummi Khan (2020) has demonstrated, being associated with BDSM sexual practice is still stigmatising, with implications for people's careers and family lives, even if there is evidently growing acceptance of the practice within the mainstream (Herbernick et al., 2021).

Conversely, scholars including Jonathan Herring (2023) and Cheryl Hanna (2001) suggest that the close elision between BDSM practice and intimate partner violence opens up the possibility that a decriminalised BDSM would provide a guise for intimate partner violence to be 'dressed up' as BDSM. To counter this, an overinclusive approach which continues to criminalise BDSM is presented as the 'least bad' approach to adopt (Hanna, 2001, p. 248, pp. 269–70). As Bradley (2023) and Monica Pa (2001) note, one of the dangers of conflating BDSM and intimate partner violence is that this erases the possibility of a consensual approach to BDSM, and moreover, situates women who participate willingly in BDSM as those responsible for the suffering of women experiencing intimate partner violence. It obfuscates the socio-cultural meaning of BDSM for those who practice it (Pa, 2001, pp. 78–9). It also hides, or silences, the voices of people who experience intimate partner violence within a relationship where there is *also* BDSM practice. It reduces their agency and their capacities to develop sexual citizenship.

Proponents of pro-BDSM positions suggest that the sort of harm that BDSM encompasses is a 'simulated' harm, not a harm in itself (Haley, 2015, p. 645), rather it is a 'parody' of violence (Pa, 2001, p. 78; Califia, 1981 [1980]). For Patrick Hopkins (1994, p. 116), it is in the possibility of negotiation, switching roles, talking about limits and establishing safe words, that BDSM becomes distinct from violence, that it becomes a simulation; it becomes 'not real harm'. Of course, as Herring (2023) might note, a bruise is still a bruise and though it may make a difference to me if my partner strangles me out of anger or for my pleasure, the impact on my body will not be vastly different. I may understand and experience both strangulations differently, but my exposure to the risk of harm is the same (Wiseman, 1997). The significance of BDSM as simulation will be important for analyses in this book, especially because, as Herring notes, it is not as simple as stating the BDSM is 'just' play or just an imitation of fantasy (2023, p. 46).

It is arousing – we want to do it – because sometimes it *does* hurt, because we want to be immersed in the erotic potentialities of sublimating and dehumanising the self, because, in the words of Charles Moser (in Moser & Madeson, 1998, p. 76), 'I am happy for the pain; I'm happy that my partner lets me be submissive … SM goes as deep as my soul'. So, though the legal status of BDSM is mostly clear, how this legal status operates, whether is it justified, whether it goes too far, or not far enough, remains a contested terrain. It is into this contestation that questions around BDSM, rough sex and what is happening when these cases come to court, emerge.

SEXUALITY AND ITS TROUBLES

Given this legal landscape, how is it that some acts of sexual violence – which in the case of Broadhurst caused the death of his partner – can successfully mobilise claims that what took place was consensual? What is happening in these cases? What do they tell us about attitudes to contemporary sexuality?

> Sexuality today is, perhaps to an unprecedented degree, a contested zone. It is more than a source of intense pleasure, or acute anxiety; it has become a moral and political battlefield … sex as pleasure, sex as sacrament, sex as a source of fulfilment, sex as fear and loathing. These issues are fought out on a terrain which is constantly extending, through the commoditisation of sexual pleasures, the spiralling expansion of potential desires, even the proliferation of sex-related dreads and diseases, and it simultaneously characterised by the emergence of new social movements and sexed subjectivities. (Weeks, 2002; 4–5)

As Jeffrey Weeks tells us, sexuality, and the way that it is governed from a socio-legal, socio-cultural perspective, is an intensely politicised terrain that is fraught with anxiety, not just about what is moral, what is good, what is good for you, but also about health, nation and what it means to be human. With so much at stake when we consider sexual expression, it is perhaps not a surprise that we might run into trouble. Trouble (verb), from the Old French verb *trubler*, means to disturb, to stir up or to make cloudy. Trouble as a noun poses problems. It causes suffering and agitation. It is obfuscatory. But it can also be an invitation. When we trouble something – encounter trouble as a verb – we destabilise it, problematise it, we challenge the certainty of the *status quo*. Troublesomeness is unsettlement, lain bare. When I am talking about sexuality as trouble in the context of rough sex and how consent is imagined and articulated within that, the effects of this troubling appear over and again.

There is, as Michel Foucault (1998 [1976]; 1982) has roundly demonstrated, nothing new about the way that the trouble of sexuality emerges. With the advent of modernity, the need to manage demographic shifts, to bolster a sense of nationhood, to encourage a self-governing, self-subjectifying citizenry, the policing of sexuality becomes a powerful site of control. As Foucault suggests, through medical, juridical, familial and educational institutions, sexuality, its expression and its conduct, has been subtly (as well as unsubtly) regulated for centuries. These are prescriptions which enshrine heteronormative, ableist, androcentric and ethnocentric power dynamics as normative, and which contribute to the construction of proscribed and necessarily deviant sexual practice. This construction of sex which is good and sex which is bad – or what Gayle Rubin (2002 [1984]) described as the charmed centre versus the outer limits – contributes, in part, to a relationship with sexuality which is anxious; which is rooted in sex negativity; that poses problems that will not be neatly solved.

The trouble posed by sexuality sometimes emerges in the thorny debates of the #MeToo movement (Fischel, 2019). It emerges in anxieties about consent education in schools, the significance of affirmative consent, and the limits of consent in establishing sexual justice (Wodda & Panfil, 2020). It emerges in the encroachment of reproductive rights. The rise of transphobic and carceral feminisms indicate potential shift in the politics of feminist or queer movements. As Khan (2016a) notes, anxiety about sex work which regulates, sanctions and in some jurisdictions, criminalises participants in these activities quite apart from any expression of consent on behalf of the sex worker, act paternalistically as moral arbiters of what women and sexual minorities should want, and should be able to do with their bodies under the law.

In England and Wales, the crisis of rape conviction rates speak for themselves. In 2022, of the 67,169 rape allegations reported to the police, just 1276 resulted in a perpetrator being charged with rape. Of these, 532 were convicted of rape. That is a conviction rate of 0.8%. These statistics have led some commentators to suggest that rape is effectively decriminalised in England and Wales (Centre for Women's Justice et al., 2020). They also tell part of the story of how contemporary rape culture which normalises violence against women and sexual minorities is nurtured (Fanghanel, 2019). This is a troubling failure of the criminal justice system. Failure, from the Latin, *fallere*, means to trip or to stumble. To miss. It is also etymologically related to 'fallacy', meaning to deceive. To fail us. However, failure, as we learn from Jack Halberstam (2011), does offer us possibility. This failure of justice is troubling, but trouble unsettles. Trouble might offer space for something more generative of possibility to emerge. Both Patrick Califia (1988) and Foucault (O'Higgins & Foucault, 1982) saw the potential of non-normative sexualities to unsettle the hegemony of contemporary sexual practice (see also Plant, 2007). When something is troubled it is destabilised. It can bring transgression. Indeed, Califia (1988) notes how transgressive the creation of pleasure can be in contexts where one does not belong. How audacious it is to create pleasure in a hostile environment. And yet, we also have to be wary of what fills this space and this potentiality for transformation: transformation into what? Who is transformed? Who is still left behind?

One of the ways that we see this tension play out is in the competing narratives around how what has come to be known as 'rough sex gone wrong' or 'sex games gone wrong' are treated in the courtroom. Through this lens, we see the failure of a criminal justice system to adequately respond to sex which employs violent themes beyond responses rooted in dominant rape myths. By attending to the interplay between consent, desire, pleasure and sexual citizenship, or how these are perceived in the courtroom, we become better able to understand this failure, better able to engage with this crisis, and more open to imagining different ways of engaging with contemporary sexuality. It will be these themes that are examined in this text.

AT THE NEXUS OF ROUGH SEX AND BDSM

It is not easy to define BDSM. Attempts to do so have been referred to as an 'exercise in futility' by some community experts (Townsend, 1983). Bondage and sadomasochism – referred to in this text by the acronym BDSM – is broad umbrella term which describes sexualised practice that employs forced themes or eroticises power imbalances. BDSM – a practice that might involve the consensual practice of restraining, whipping, hitting, humiliating, choking, subjugating a partner (Sowersby et al., 2022, p. 2; Haley, 2015, p. 634) – has been described as a means through which to resignify pain within a consensual context (Khan, 2014, p. 10), to explore different levels of kinkiness (Haley, 2015, p. 634), or express sexual citizenship outside the strictures of conventional sexual expression (Moran, 2017 [1995]). Commentators have demonstrated that some of the key elements of BDSM which distinguish these practices from assault or unwanted violence are the roles of consent, communication and voluntariness in the practice (Jozifkova, 2013; Fanghanel, 2020; Williams et al., 2014). Martin S. Weinberg et al. (1984, pp. 380–1) identify five features that comprise sadomasochistic activity: the interplay between dominance and submission; role play; consent; a sexual context; and what they call a 'mutual definition' of what partners are doing – a shared understanding that *this is BDSM*.

According to Bente Træen and colleagues (2021) within a Norwegian context, up to a third of adults might have experimented with BDSM themes; a practice which until 2013 was deemed a pathology by the Diagnostic and Statistical Manual of Mental Disorders (DSM) (a key tool for the classification of psychiatric disorders) (Singy, 2012; Khan, 2014). The increased awareness about, and mainstreaming of, BDSM practice can, in part, be attributed to its appearance in mainstream cultural texts (Khan, 2014; Pa 2001). Notwithstanding its declassification as a mental disorder, analysis of the mainstreaming of BDSM points to the way in which BDSM practice is rarefied or reinterpreted in a way that has tendency to intrinsically link BDSM to mental disorder or pathology (Khan, 2014; Weiss; 2006; Wilkinson, 2009). Moreover, the visions of BDSM that we are shown in cultural representations – in films, music videos, advertising – are either idealised, almost sanitised visions of BDSM in which people are glamourous, alluring and powerful, or they are ridiculous objects of mockery (Fanghanel, 2019). As Califia states, 'at MTV level, S/M looks more acceptable. The reality, for actual perverts, is that it's not' (cited in Pa, 2001, p. 55). And yet, as Khan (2014) demonstrates, no matter how incomplete they are, these visions of BDSM in the mainstream matter because they come to inform how BDSM is understood. For the purposes of this book, these constructions of BDSM will, as we will see, inform how rough sex is dealt with in court.

Rough sex, or a sex game gone wrong, encompasses many elements that connect it with BDSM. Rough sex has been defined by Rebecca L. Burch and Catherine Salmon (2019, p. 386) as comprising hair pulling, biting, being tied up and slapping. The similarity with definitions of BDSM is clear, and yet, rough sex and BDSM are not straightforwardly the same thing. For some practitioners of BDSM, this sexual subculture is considered to be a fundamental part of who they are (Haley, 2015; Moser & Madeson, 1998); it is their sexuality. BDSM expression is how they become fully sexual citizens (Weeks, 1998; Stychin, 2001). Indeed, BDSM has been compared to other ritualistic practices and so it is not difficult to fathom the significance that BDSM can play in the forging of some subjectivities (Sagarin et al., 2015). For other BDSM-ers, the practice is much less intrinsic to their sense of self, but is nonetheless, a deliberate, chosen endeavour. They might identify as being drawn to elements of the subculture, its paraphernalia, its vernacular, its community (Weiss, 2011; Fanghanel, 2019). Rough sex, on the other hand, is more likely to be what I term as BDSM-adjacent. It borrows from the subcultural practices of BDSM without necessarily buying into the cosmology of BDSM praxis. For Emily A. Vogels and Lucia F. O'Sullivan (2019), a salient distinction between BDSM and rough sex is that rough sex comprises sexual activity, whereas BDSM, though erotic, does not necessarily have to include sex. Self-awareness, or self-identification as a BDSM practitioner is also a salient distinction, here.

Herring posits that one of the complexities of BDSM practice lies in this adjacency. The sliding around between BDSM and rough sex might be at the root of the impasse that we encounter. For Herring, BDSM is too conceptually close to the ongoing 'phenomenon of violence against women and girls' (2023, p. 47) and provides too adequate a cover for intimate partner violence. Certainly, in some of the cases that we shall encounter in this book, this is true. Herring levels a further critique against BDSM; BDSM lacks political awareness. In re-enacting slave auctions, scenes of torture in Guantanamo Bay or playing out rape fantasies, BDSM rehearses the anguish of oppressed people without unsettling the abuses of power that enable them (see Weiss, 2009). I posit that no sexual practice is apolitical, as we will see in chapters to come, however the potential for complacency within BDSM subcultures – or even complicity with oppression and marginalisation – is evident (see Fanghanel, 2019).

When it comes to the rough sex defence, it is even more important to eradicate this complacency. The slipperiness of concepts like BDSM and rough sex, the conflation of BDSM with intimate partner violence, the criminalisation and condonement of some aspects of BDSM practice are troublesome both for pro-BDSM campaigners and for those seeking to protect women from being killed or injured by men in a so-called sex game gone wrong. This is one of the complexities that campaigners for the liberalisation in law of BDSM sexual practice need to reckon with. It is a circumstance facilitated by the elisions made between BDSM and BDSM-adjacent sex. It is also an expression of how sexuality troubles as much as it can be troubled.

In this book, I walk the line between the imperative to protect minority sexual rights and sexual agency on the one hand, and the imperative to prevent defendants from raising a revamped 'she asked for it' defence in court. The socio-legal status quo in which we find ourselves here does a disservice to everyone.

ENCOUNTERING THE SPECTACULAR

The blurring of these categories is made possible through the spectacularisation of sexual practice. Guy Debord mobilises the concept of the spectacle to explain a form of atomisation in contemporary social life. For Debord, the spectacle – all-consuming, self-perpetuating, tautological – is a technique of obfuscation which turns truth and falseness on their heads. Spectacularisation is a form of fragmentation in which what is 'real' and what is 'spectacular' transforms human social life. The notion of the spectacle describes an alienation process whereby what is spectacularised comes to stand in for, and be indistinguishable from, the 'real', all the while not being 'real'. It is 'fetishised pure objectivity' and becomes a commodity (Debord, 2021 [1967], p. 7). When human social – here we might add sexual – life is spectacularised, its composition is obscured. This means that we cannot readily perceive the composition of that life: what composes it? What exploits it? What does it assume, or consume, or resist?

Debord notes that one of the reasons why the spectacular is such a beguiling success is that it 'presents itself as a vast, inaccessible reality that can never be questioned'. It becomes, in the words of Bruno Latour (1987), 'black boxed'. Black boxed concepts are ones that appear easy to use, but where that ease comes from a refusal to, or an inability to, interrogate how those concepts are made; what comprises them. Their murky complexity becomes obscured. The consequences of this are that passivity is 'demanded' from the spectacle, it can never be interrogated, its composition can never be fully understood, and as a result, people living lives that are spectacularised – mediated, not 'real' – can never fully exist. Fully existing, fully engaging with one's existing, is an ethos which underpins the politics of sexual citizenship rights. That which is spectacularised is isolating, manipulative, and disables critique whilst fostering benign comfort in the *status quo*; not troubling it. For Debord, everything has become spectacle, and in the chapters that follow we will explore in more detail the ways in which consent, bondage and sex positivity have all become spectacularised, and what this means for socially, sexually just outcomes.

'Everything that was directly lived has receded into a spectacle,' Debord tells us (2021 [1967], p. 1). In this book, I will demonstrate that consent, BDSM and desire are concepts that, in the socio-legal realm, become spectacularised events. This separation between the sign and the thing signified creates a new reality that is both fully real and fully false. Debord calls this a 'reciprocal alienation', which self-devouringly consumes the distinction between the thing and the thing copied; 'what appears is good; what is good appears' (Debord, 2021 [1967], p. 4). It presides over a social passivity which does not – *which cannot* – be questioned. In the context of socio-legal approaches to rough sex, the operation of the spectacular is even more disquieting. Because the spectacle gives the illusion of reality, it also professes authentic objectivity. The impartiality of the judiciary is at the bedrock of modern, contemporary legal systems around the globe. If rough sex cases rely on concepts which are spectacularised, then the objectivity of those concepts is both taken for granted and negated. This objectivity is fetishised (Debord, 2021 [1967], p. 7) and in this abstraction, presents a reality that is both illusory and ready to be consumed.

This talk of abstraction and obfuscation necessarily recalls Jean Baudrillard's discussion of simulacra where, as with the spectacle, the simulacra are 'true' (1994, p. 1). Not a representation of a sign, not a preference of 'the sign over the thing signified' which is where Debord starts from, the simulacrum 'substitutes the sign of the real for the real'. The sign is real. We do not spectate the illusion; the illusion is real and we are in it. We are party, willingly, to our own mystification. This mystification – this enchantment – to borrow (ish) from Max Weber, fosters the hyperreal. Here, for Baudrillard, society is so fully composed of simulacra that these 'unreal reals' take on a life of their own, becoming more real than the reality they sign to. Hyperreality obliterates what is real and turns 'the real into a satellite' (2017 [1976], p. 95), entirely fragmenting it, whilst also taking its place. Baudrillard offers us the example of Disneyland or of the Watergate scandal as examples of hyperreality; both microcosms which reflect and replace a simulation whilst becoming more 'real' than what they represent. Over the next few chapters, we will see how hyperreality can be perceived in discourses mobilised in rough sex cases. It is important to remember that what is hyperreal is both real and not real; simultaneously actually, a meaningful, sensible representation and also the simulation of one. What was real is no longer possible in a spectacularised simulated social context. When we see how this manifests in socio-legal discourse, this therefore means that we may well say 'but it is isn't like that!' or 'that's not true', but these objections will almost not matter because in the context where hyperreality emerges, it is endlessly true, and endlessly 'like that'. I say that it 'almost' does not matter, because of course, once we see the spectacle, once we understand the hyperreal, we might acquire the exteriority that will be necessary to critique this status quo and to respond to the trouble that sexuality makes for us.

SEEING THE SPECTACLE

The data that this book uses are gleaned from analyses of court case transcripts. I wanted to understand how consent is construed in these cases and the attempts to demonstrate that consent to violence during a sexual encounter was present.

In order to do this work, I identified, using legal databases such as The Law Pages, Westlaw and LexisNexis, cases where a defence of consent is raised in the case of a sex game gone wrong. Using key search terms including 'rough sex', 'sex game gone wrong', 'BDSM', 'bondage', 'sadomasochism' and 'sado-masochism', I was able to collect an array of cases from the past twenty years. Both LexisNexis and Westlaw hold cases from the Court of Appeal, only.

A limitation with using these databases to search for cases is that they only report cases that go to appeal. Cases where there is no appeal, or where the defendant is found not guilty, are not reported here. To try to plug this gap, I conducted a media search, using the same search terms, for cases reported about in the press. Using LexisNexis for this too, I was able to access 3400 news reports from 1988 to 2023 about rough sex, sadomasochism and sex games gone wrong. Reading these, I was able to create a more complete database of cases that might be relevant. Of course, this overlooks cases which are not reported in the press. Finally, I triangulated the list I had compiled with the list WCCTT were also putting together at the same moment, excluding cases which do not take place in the jurisdiction of England and Wales.

In order to examine and compare similarities and differences across these cases, including the way in which they are gendered, cases were then organised by different categories where a rough sex defence is raised: women killed by men; men killed by women (of which there was one); men killed by men (I found nine, including men who kill themselves either deliberately or by accident); women killed by women (of which there were none). Even this initial sorting of data demonstrates how sex games which have gone wrong are a gendered crime. Women are disproportionately the victim, and men are usually the offenders (Edwards, 2015; 2017; Yardley, 2021).

Though transcripts of these Court of Appeal cases are readily available to read, they do not tell us enough about the existence, or not, of consent. To better understand this aspect, it would be the Crown Court transcripts that I would need. Speaking to the Crown Courts, it became clear that it would not be possible to acquire transcripts dating from before 2010, so I limited my analysis to cases taking place between 2010 and 2023. A total of thirteen cases were identified where death had occurred and thirteen where injury had occurred. I was able to acquire the transcript of the summing up or sentencing remarks of eleven cases involving deaths, and three where injury occurred. Other cases were not available either because data was lost or permission to acquire transcripts was not granted.

There is also a significant cost implication to conducting research using court transcripts in England and Wales. It is not always easy to obtain transcripts, and the barriers to access – though not the focus of this book – should be a cause for concern for scholars, activists and people preoccupied with justice concerns more broadly. Transcripts range in length from nine pages to over 100 pages. The average length of case was 34.2 pages. If some cases appear more frequently or at greater length than others in what follows, this is, in part, because of the different volumes of data that I was able to acquire in different cases. Though the cases analysed in this text are only a small part of the overall picture of how this phenomenon emerges, the analysis enables us to understand them as a microcosm of social–cultural approaches to sexual justice beyond the microcosm. Other than barriers to access, a limitation of using court transcripts to analyse how concepts such as consent, sadomasochism or sex positivity are constructed in court is that the transcripts can be incomplete. Incorrectly heard words or inaudible material can confuse the meaning of what the transcripts says. This is a risk with all transcribed material, but here, a researcher using court transcripts is more removed from the primary source of what was said in court than they tend to be from focus groups, interviewees or other sources of empirical data, which makes it harder to mitigate against these confusions or omissions.

The question about what to do about anonymising cases analysed in research like this is a vexed one (Gavey, 2024). Some scholars decide to completely anonymise cases that they use (Milne, 2021). Others, like me, decide not to do this. You will find that most of the cases in this book are not anonymised. For me, it is important to name women who have been killed by men and to name the men too. Naming humanises women in these cases, and helps to acknowledge what has happened in them. Most of the cases that are analysed in this book are reported about in the press, and so the stories are in the public domain. They can all be searched for on publicly accessible databases. Where women have not been killed, their names are anonymised in court transcripts (and so are here too). I grappled with the ethics of analysing cases where men were found guilty of no crime (there are four of these in this book) and I decided to retain these cases because they tell us more about how consent 'works' in these cases, which is important in a context where consent is no defence to injury sustained for sexual gratification. Because defendants have been found not guilty in these cases, they and the names of the complainants/victims have been anonymised. I sought and received appropriate permissions from the courts who own the copyright of their transcripts to reproduce them here. One of the criticisms levelled at the way that female victims are treated in court is that their character is traduced. These cases are really no exception to that, so the decision to use real names in these cases is not one that is taken lightly. I am aware of the real, ongoing pain that these crimes will have caused these women and the people who know and love them, and I am aware that writing about them here is difficult, in that regard. Yet, the violences enacted on these women in court has been real. What I want to do is to expose that violence to move towards better sexual justice. I want to pay tribute to women in each of these cases, and women like them who have also been killed or injured during an apparently consensual sexual encounter.

From the beginning, I wanted to understand, in the Broadhurst case for instance, how the court 'knew' that Connolly had consented to elements of what took place on the night that she had died. It was necessary to examine the text of the transcripts themselves, to conduct a thematic and discourse analysis of the language used, to excavate how knowledge of consent is constructed. To conduct this analysis, I read the cases several times, noting moments of significance, how evidence is presented to tell a story about the events of the case, and the assumptions that underpin the internal logic of what is said. I also noted the order in which topics were spoken about and how presenting certain facts before, after or alongside others worked to set the scene about what had unfolded, and how. Often the structuring of these observations made by the judge also painted a picture that would be based on normative assumptions about gender, desire, morality and sexuality.

One of the obvious and important limitations of using court transcripts in this way is that they reduce the events, and the people involved in them, into two-dimensional figures who exist only in the moments of these crimes. The victims in the cases analysed in this book all too often no longer have their own voices to tell their own stories, and in my rendering of how these crimes are framed in court, I have tried to present them fully, with compassion and humanity. However, given what we are told from these transcripts and given how women's lives, desires and experiences are put to work (often against them) to help to tell stories about rough sex, these are partial, fragmented flattenings of the women. It is an ironic spectacularisation of women and also the men in these cases. This is not what I wanted, and it has troubled me that it is an artefact of using court transcripts to conduct analysis. So why persist, when more feminist methodological approaches were probably available? There is an obvious authority to what judges say in court, so even if the renderings of the actors are rarefied, they are crucial to understanding the operation of justice. In order to understand more about how rough sex is treated in court and why it is treated in this way, it is necessary to look at what has happened in the court. That the artefacts themselves result in the rarefication of victims is an act of violence and dehumanisation, but it is important for us to see that this is happening as this is another way that troubling sexuality is spectacularised. These are themes that I revisit throughout the book.

Ultimately, in many cases that were analysed, consent is not explicitly evidenced. Instead, the existence of consent is merely stated as fact – a Debordian 'we know she consented because she consented'. The fact of consent is rarely questioned. In order to delve more deeply into analyses of what is being consented to, how we know there was consent, and what this consent looked like, it became necessary to look for evidence of how consent was operationalised by the defence. Rather like a black hole, because we cannot see the consent, we have to look around it to find clues that it is present, or that it is not. Consent does quite a lot of work in these cases, and rather like the black hole whose gravitational pull draws everything into it, its takes on an outsized significance in many of the cases that are analysed in this book. A Latourian black box, consent is not interrogated, we cannot see it, and we do not know what it comprises anyway. What follows over the next few chapters is an exposition of how the so-called rough sex defence can work, even as it is simultaneously condemned, criticised and still impossible in law in many jurisdictions.

STRUCTURE OF THE BOOK

The themes running through these cases will show that they are not special cases, but rather iterations of stories that we already know about gendered justice. This book considers, in turn, how BDSM, consent, and sex positivity are figured in cases where a rough sex 'defence' is raised. These are the three principal themes that have emerged from this analysis of the cases. Before doing that, in the next chapter, I explore contemporary sexual landscapes. Drawing on feminist commentary about the evolution of sexual politics, I outline how distinct theoretical approaches contribute to the socio-cultural landscape that non-normative sexual practice finds itself in now. A landscape that casts sex as exceptional, consent as enchanting, and non-normativity as troubling. To do this, I consider how this contemporary landscape creates the conditions for consent, sexual agency, integrity and desire to be spectacularised. Here, I also present the cases that are examined in this text.

As some of the discussion in this opening chapter demonstrates, debates about consent are at the heart of BDSM and rough sex debates. Chapter 3 establishes how consent is currently understood both in law and then at a socio-cultural level. It will establish what consent looks like in cases where consensual BDSM or rough sex may be taking place, whilst also establishing the limits of consent. It will detail the ways in which consent is upheld as the gold standard of ethical sexual practice both within the BDSM community and beyond it. It will critically interrogate this claim, to demonstrate that in certain circumstances, consent is not enough. Or rather, consent does not do the work that we think it does. The chapter then turns to analyses of court cases where a defence of consent is raised. It examines how consent is evidenced or claimed in these cases – what consent looks like – and then considers the extent to which these expressions of consent are spectacularised. This spectacularisation mobilises a problematically idealised vision of the forms that consent takes in rough sex encounters.

Many of the cases that I have analysed for this text rely on stereotypical tropes borrowed from BDSM subcultures to make their argument. Chapter 4 examines how some aspects of BDSM cultures have entered the mainstream imaginary and how this understanding of BDSM is used to account for what happens in a context where rough sex 'goes wrong'. Detailing the rise of a so-called 'rough sex defence' or 'consent defence' over the past few decades, this chapter posits that some aspects of BDSM have become more acceptable in the mainstream, and this is why claims of consent are more readily mobilised. These partial – and spectacularised – visions of BDSM are heteronormative and deeply gendered. More than this, the mobilisation of them is a disservice to BDSM communities and BDSM practitioners, and they facilitate gendered violence.

In the penultimate chapter of this book, I examine the role that sex positivity plays, here. In part, a more permissive sexual attitude has facilitated BDSM tropes entering the mainstream, and this might also herald a move towards a more sex positive attitude within a socio-legal setting. This chapter examines cases where sex positivity appears to emerge, what discourses and power dynamics it relies on, and importantly, whether it is, indeed, sex positive. It argues that sex positivity is spectacularised. Instead, what emerges is a twist on established rape myths which enshrine rape culture in contemporary society.

Not all violence harms in the same way. The final chapter of this book revisits the productive and degenerative concept of sexuality in trouble and the spectacle. It argues that in contemporary cases where consent to sexual violence is used as a defence, consent, BDSM and sex positivity are constructed and expressed as an instrument of violence. They foster a rape culture which normalises gendered violence. Of course, the concept of violence has a double role in this chapter. Here, I still hold space for violence that is wanted and consented to in the context of a knowing and deliberate BDSM encounter. The space for this activity is eroded in contemporary legal discourse even as violence is also facilitated by contemporary attitudes to rough sex in court. The work that rape myths and rape culture do here is not to be underestimated. The violence addressed in this chapter is not only that which is wanted and that which is not; the chapter also exposes the violence of the law, the violence of consent discourses and the violence of the spectacular. This final chapter calls for de-exceptionalism and disenchantment as tools with which to encounter these troubles and to transcend these impasses.

2. Spectacular Sexual Landscapes

The cases analysed in this book reflect a microcosm of the socio-cultural context in which they exist. Understanding the politics of these moments helps us perceive issues of sexual justice and identify how they operate against a broader background of rape culture. Though they are artefacts of contemporary contexts, these microcosms also help to constitute sexual politics more broadly. That is, they are both products of a socio-cultural past and present *and* they are productive of it. Through these debates, and throughout these cases, key concepts emerge which reflect and constitute a sexual status quo. In order to better understand what these are, and the impact that they have on contemporary sexual justice, it is helpful to examine the sexual landscape in which we find ourselves.

Here, this chapter provides a brief overview of this sexual landscape. Beginning with an account of the genealogy of BDSM as a socio-cultural concern, I turn to the distinction between BDSM and the BDSM-adjacent, or 'rough sex', that is at the centre of many of the cases that I analyse. I then give an account of the legal position of BDSM in England and Wales, the USA and Canada; jurisdictions where much of the scholarship that I draw on about BDSM and its legal status emerges. I then examine a feminist history of debates about consent, pornography, rough sex and BDSM (known, reductively, as the 'sex wars'). The roles of sex positivity and sexual exceptionalism are then considered, before finishing with a consideration of enchantment and what it does to our understanding of contemporary sexuality. Finally, the cases that are analysed in this book are presented in turn.

In Chapter 1, I posited that contemporary sexual politics are troubled. This trouble is not new, as historians of sexuality have demonstrated. Sexual practice, sexual desire and sexuality itself have long been sites of anxiety, control and resistance in the post-industrialist global north, where the scenes of the cases addressed in this book play out (Foucault, 1982; Weeks, 2002; Krafft-Ebing, 2011 [1894]). The imperative to observe, scrutinise, sanction, covet, desire sexual practice has an ancestry that is well-known. The original text of Richard von Krafft-Ebing's *Psychopathia Sexualis* dates from 1886 and comprises a veritable near Borgesian heterotopia of sexual proclivities, fetishes and disorders which served to inform medical and psychological knowledge about sexual pathologies.

Perhaps one of the most well-known sexual 'deviants' in the history of sexuality studies is the individual whose name is given to one element of the 'sadomasochism' compound. Donatien Alphonse François de Sade was first imprisoned for his involvement in sexual scandals and for the lewdness of his erotic writings in 1777. Not unlike Krafft-Ebing's taxonomy of sexual deviancy, Sade's more notorious work, '120 Days of Sodom', reads like a catalogue of debauchery, making it a surprisingly ludicrous read for even enthusiasts of his libertine aesthetics. Against this background, it is not unexpected that an obsession with sexual practice has placed sexuality, in the main, as trouble to be solved through sanction; and I mean sanction in all senses of the contranym.

WHAT IS BDSM?

The cases that are examined in this book all concern instances where women have been killed or injured by men during a sexual encounter. In each of these cases, a claim that what took place during that encounter was consensual, or wanted, is raised. Within political, media and popular discourses around these cases, this is sometimes referred to as a 'consent defence' or a 'rough sex defence'. There is a relationship between these rough sexual encounters and the potentially more codified BDSM that can also encompass rough themes. Before unpacking what is really at stake in these defence claims, it is helpful to consider how we got here. What does the landscape where such a claim could have currency look like?

In these cases, women are injured with whips, chains or other instruments used to hit them. They are forced into sexual penetration as part of 'rape play' fantasies. They are branded. They are killed by strangulation with hands, ropes or belts. Sometimes they are stabbed in the neck. Sometimes they are beaten so badly that they die of their injuries. Sometimes they are set on fire. And as horrific as this list of abuses sounds, sometimes, some women, not these women, will have sought out something like these practices as an expression of sadomasochistic sexual desire.

That these practices – beating, choking, branding – appear within some forms of sadomasochist practice means that when these cases appear in court, they rely on BDSM-like themes to be comprehensible as potentially mitigating claims. Parties in the cases analysed in this book may not specifically recognise what they do as BDSM, but as we will see, what they *do* do does borrow significantly from established BDSM themes. Rough sex is not the same as BDSM, and this distinction is important, but they are cognate with each other. It is worth exploring this intersect between BSDM and 'rough sex' – or what I have called 'BDSM-adjacent' sex – to better understand what is going on here when these claims enter the courtroom.

As we began to see in the Chapter 1, over recent decades there has been a proliferation in the body of research that examines BDSM practice and exposes analysis of this subculture within the mainstream. BDSM, or sadomasochism, can refer to a practice or a subculture in which themes of force, domination and submission play out in an eroticised context. BDSM can include practices as diverse as whipping, spanking, restraining, role play, simulated threats, verbal or physical humiliation, and other acts of control (see Pa, 2001; Newmahr, 2011; Weiss, 2011). Various niches emerge within the subculture, including age play, knife play, breath play, encounters using bodily fluids (urine, faeces), pet play. Patrick Califia (1981 [1980], p. 168) describes the 'charm' of 'frightful reveries' as a 'private world of dominance, submission, punishment and pain'. With its stylised aesthetics, safe words, imperatives around negotiation and aftercare, BDSM comprises a subculture which exists within, is constituted by, and influential of, a non-BDSM – vanilla, perhaps – mainstream (Fanghanel, 2019; Dunkley & Brotto, 2020).

It is hard to be prescriptive about what counts as BDSM, but we do have some clues. According to Martin S. Weinberg et al. (1984), people who practice BDSM tend to read BDSM-related material and magazines, attend social events related to BDSM practice, and buy, or make BDSM paraphernalia. If Weinberg et al. were writing in the 2020s, they might add having a profile on BDSM-related social media or following BDSM blogs could indicate a BDSM-inclined identity or interest of sorts. Thus, BDSM practice can be seen to emerge as a subculture. Not everyone who is a BDSM practitioner might attend events or consider themselves to be part of a BDSM community, but there are likely to be shared interests in some of these themes in their lives. Additionally, for Weinberg et al. (1984, pp. 380–1), BDSM comprises domination and submission – power play – roleplay, consent, a sexual meaning – an understanding that what is happening is erotically charged – and a shared understanding of the practice as BDSM.

According to the campaign group SM Gays, building on the work of Larry Townsend (1983), BDSM activity comprises a dom/sub relationship, the giving and receiving of pain that is pleasurable, role play, the conscious humbling of one partner by the other, elements of fetish, and ritualised flagellation (2002). Explicit reference to consent does not make the cut here, but reference to acts which are conscious or pleasurable speak to practices which are *wanted* and *deliberate*.

Clearly, a key aspect of BDSM is the consensual element of the practice. The public face of BDSM is replete with emphasis on precisely how intrinsic consent in BDSM. As D. J. Williams et al. (2014) demonstrate in their tour of how the centrality of consent is articulated, comparing various acronyms used as practical frameworks to underpin 'correct BDSM' practice, consent is at the centre. Starting with the proposition that BDSM should be SSC (safe, sane and consensual), through to (and eschewing the stigmatising imperative to be 'sane') RACK (risk aware consensual kink), Williams et al. (2014) offer the 4Cs as a framework – BDSM that centres caring, communication, consent and caution. These iterations place consent at the heart of sexual practice at every turn, and yet, as Williams et al. (2014) also note, consent is tricky. The authors suggest that consent be thought of as a multilayered interplay between 'surface consent' – the yes/no means yes/no consent – 'scene consent' – what will happen in the encounter, what the safe word will be, and 'deep consent' – what is really going on? Does the submissive want their boundaries to be pushed? Are they in distress even though they have not 'safe-worded' yet? This nuanced approach to consent understands the limits of 'she didn't say no' consent and captures some of the co-constituted intersubjective richness of consent that is implied in its etymology – 'con sentir': *coming together to feel*.

Consent, in this form, is suffused with willing, with voluntariness, with communication and with awareness that what is going on is BDSM of some sort. BDSM is characterised by being informed, unfrightened and unashamed (unless this is what practitioners want). Whether it takes place in a group, or alone, with costumes, with implements, with toys, at home or in a club, as part of a community, or as a community outsider, whether it ends in orgasm or not, whether you take your clothes off or not, whether it involves genital touching or not, BDSM has qualities which cast it outside the realm of an abusive relationship or other form of offence against the person (Jozifkova, 2013; Pitagora, 2013; Wodda and Panfil 2020, 2021). Indeed, for Terry Hoople (1996), non-consensual or abusive practice that looks like BDSM would not be considered BDSM by the BDSM community. Abusive men would find themselves without submissives to play with because they would not have earned the 'right', or be worthy enough, to dominate a partner.

This is not to say, by any means, that abuse does not take place within BDSM practice. Consent can be violated, boundaries can be crossed, bad behaviour can masquerade as play for the purposes of getting away with it (Fanghanel, 2019; Dunkley & Brotto, 2020; Walling-Wefelmeyer & O'Neill, 2021). Though there are good intentions behind the centrality of consent within BDSM practice, consent is in practice, as I have intimated above, difficult to deal with. The intersubjective power dynamics – often cut along intersectional axes of identity such as ethnicity, ability, class, age and gender – impact on different actors' actual capacity to freely consent to sexual practice or, indeed to safe-word, or to withdraw their consent, or have those refusals recognised (Jozifkova, 2013, p. 392; Dunkley & Brotto, 2020). What these accounts do for us, however, is provide a tentative blueprint for how we might identify BDSM when we come across it.

All of this is crucial because, when so-called 'sex games gone wrong' cases reach the courtroom, the claims often lean on distorted or imagined perceptions of BDSM to gain credibility. By understanding what BDSM practitioners believe their practices *should* embody, we can subject such claims to sharper, more informed scrutiny.

These characteristics of BDSM must be held alongside what we 'know' about rough sex. Certainly not all BDSM has what we might conventionally understand as 'sex' as part of it, but BDSM-esque tropes do appear in how rough sex cases are spoken about in court.

WHAT IS ROUGH SEX?

The language in the cases that are analysed in this book all use concepts of 'rough sex', 'sex games gone wrong' and 'sadomasochism' more or less interchangeably. As I have started to indicate, whilst the distinction between these different concepts might not be made – and may not even matter – in these cases, they are conceptually distinct practices. Rough sex, suggest Chelsea-Jade Sowersby et al. (2022, p. 2) comprises sexual practice 'involving a degree of force or aggression' that is nonetheless consensual. Rough sex borrows from themes of BDSM – the 'restraining, choking, slapping' – which is why it can be understood as 'adjacent' to BDSM. Emily A. Vogels and Catherine O'Sullivan (2019), Debby Herbernick et al. (2021) and Sowersby et al. (2022) all suggest that pornography, the ease with which it can be accessed, and the increased representation of violence within pornographic materials normalises aggression in sexual encounters (see Vera-Gray et al., 2021). This surge in the accessibility of pornography may play a part in the proliferation of people who appear to engage BDSM or BDSM-adjacent themes in their sexual practices. Nicola Gavey (2024, p. 5) suggests that this proliferation contributes to a 'discourse of the modern mythology of everyday kink'. That is, that BDSM-adjacent practices are common, that this is how people – especially young people – have sex these days, that the 'everydayness' of kink is an expression of hetero-sexy agentic sexual self-determination (Dobson, 2011; Gavey, 2024, p. 7). Gavey notes in her work analysing trial transcripts that despite their distinctions, rough sex, sex games gone wrong and BDSM are conflated in legal discourses, sliding around each other in an 'ethical vacuum' (Gavey, 2024, p. 8). This means that practices such that 'sexual domination … spanking, hair-pulling, double penetration', thus become spectacularised in their own way, and divorced from the specific sexual subculture of BDSM (Herbernick et al., 2021, p. 1184). For Jonathan Herring, rough sex is that which 'would normally be seen as aggressive, painful or an assault' (2023, p. 34). More than this, Herring suggests that rough sex is a type of sex that needs 'specific consent beyond a general consent to have sex'. Thus, as with BDSM, consent is the critical piece of the encounter which distinguishes a 'sex game' or 'rough sex' from assault. Rough sex and sex games will typically involve sex, whilst BDSM practice might not necessarily comprise any activity that could be typically recognised as sex (Burch & Salmon, 2019, p. 384).

As Weinberg et al. (1984) posit above, a constituent feature of BDSM is that all parties 'know' that they are doing BDSM. Whilst, as Burch and Salmon (2019, p. 390) demonstrate, rough sex is something that participants engage in, mutually initiate and find enjoyable, the accoutrements of BDSM practice about negotiation, aftercare, safe words and so on are less prevalent. Studies of rough sex have tended towards examining how participants understand the sex that they are having, what they do, who with and why, and less on these other safeguarding elements around communication, care and consent negotiations, even though these may also be taking place (Herbernick et al., 2021).

Thus, we see significant crossover between BDSM and rough sex in terms of what people do. There are possibly differences between how they think about what they do. That these concepts skate over each other, sometimes imperceptibly, has two potential implications for questions of sexual justice. Firstly, as we will come to see in the next section, consensual BDSM – a tautological phrase – is criminalisable in nearly all jurisdictions. Advocates for the rights of BDSM practitioners to conduct their sexual practice without fear of criminalisation argue that the continued bar on the ability to consent to sexual practices which cause non-life-threatening injuries, for instance, is an infringement of their sexual rights, their sexual citizenship and their right to a private life (Haley, 2015; Onoma, 2017). Secondly, alongside this, some elements of BDSM subculture are penetrating the mainstream. The legitimacy of BDSM as something to desire in and of itself has gained more traction. Therefore, we see elements of BDSM practice in mainstream spaces including the courtroom. Yet, those representations, divorced from knowledge about the history, culture and ethos of the subculture, mean that they are reified glimpses of BDSM that penetrate the mainstream. This matters for advocates for the rights of BDSM practitioners because of the potential to mislead about what doing/being BDSM means for those people within that subculture.

I posit that the mainstreaming of BDSM subculture has contributed to the increased incidences of consent claims being raised in court. It is also true that the increased visibility and availability of pornographic representations of rough sex and BDSM-adjacent acts might also contribute to this climate. Even here, however, the slide of BDSM imagery into mainstream pornography is one that is marked by the increased acceptability of BDSM as a practice, fuelling, yes, the 'myth of everyday kink' (Gavey, 2024).

When BDSM is understood as a legitimate desire in this way, its spectacularised representation in court cases can be used to excuse, condone or mitigate actions which, without these understandings of BDSM subculture in its full complexity, enable bad behaviour to masquerade as BDSM in an attempt to 'get away with it'. This has implications, both for the justice outcomes of victims of crimes associated with rough sex or BDSM and for BDSM practitioners themselves. Examining the contemporary legal landscape of consent, rough sex and BDSM will help us better understand this tension.

BDSM IN ENGLAND AND WALES

The law in England and Wales is clear about whether or not it is possible to consent to injury sustained during the course of a sadomasochistic encounter. (It is not possible.) The case which establishes this principle is the well-known case of *R* v. *Brown* (1993) in which the House of Lords – then the highest court in the country – held that it is not possible to consent to sadomasochistic acts: 'which inflicted injuries which were neither transient or trifling, notwithstanding that the acts were committed in private, the person on whom the injuries were inflicted consented to the acts, and no permanent injury was sustained' (*R* v. *Brown*, 1993, p. 1).

The facts of *Brown* are well known. It concerns a group of men who were involved in sadomasochistic practice with each other. The activities that took place between them occurred mostly in private, including in the homes of some of the men. Activities were recorded using video tape and were then shared amongst the group. These videos were intercepted by police who, launching Operation Spanner, set about trying to find the men in the videos and, convinced that they had come across some snuff pornography (a form of pornography which depicts the death of somebody), dug up the gardens of some of the men, looking for bodies. No bodies were discovered, though forty men were arrested in the course of Operation Spanner. Sixteen were charged and found guilty of assault occasioning actual bodily harm (Moran, 2017 [1995], p. 225; SM Gays, 2002). The men claimed that what they were doing could not be assaultive because everybody who participated had consented to what happened. In the House of Lords decision, Lord Templeman stated: 'I am not prepared to invent a defence of consent for sado-masochistic encounters which breed and glorify cruelty and result in offences under ss 47 and 20 of the 1861 Act' (*R* v. *Brown*, 1993, p. 8).

Thus – and making exception for 'manly diversions' such as violent sports, boxing or wrestling, along with 'surgical operations, sports, the chastisement of children, jostling in a crowd, but all subject to a reasonable degree of force being used, tattooing and ear-piercing' (53) – consent is not a defence to injury in cases of sadomasochism. This case has been widely analysed and critiqued by socio-legal scholars for its homophobic undertones (Moran, 2017 [1995]; Stychin, 1995; Ashford, 2010; Cowan, 2010), its sex negativity (Pa, 2001; Khan, 2014), and its over-reliance on stereotypes of sadomasochistic sex (as an 'uncivilised' and 'evil thing' (*R* v. *Brown*, 1993, p. 9; see also Hoople, 1996). It is not, perhaps, necessary to unpack all of the different ways in which this judgment has been analysed from different perspectives to highlight the assumptions that underpin the decision, as these are well explored elsewhere. Rather, for the purposes of this discussion, in the context of the cases analysed in this book, it is helpful to note that despite its heterocentrism, despite its over-reliance on idealised and demonised construction of masculinity, despite its homophobia and sex negativity, and the way the judges' comments serve to constitute gay BDSMers as 'unpredictably dangerous', 'degrading' and 'barbaric' sexual outsiders (*R* v. *Brown*, 1993, p. 7), this is the law in England and Wales: whether it is BDSM, rough sex or a sex game, there is no defence of consent to injury sustained during a consensual sexual encounter.

In 1997, four years after the final judgments in Brown were passed, the House of Lords considered the 1996 case of *R* v. *Wilson*. This case, too, featured BDSM-like practice and questions of consent. Alan Wilson was charged with – and at the Court of Appeal found guilty of – assault occasioning actual bodily harm for using a hot knife to brand his initials onto the buttocks of his wife, an act which we are told was at her 'instigation'. This branding needed medical treatment, and it was the wife's doctor who reported the injury to the police.

Wilson's evidence to the police was read out in court:

> She wanted a tattoo, and I didn't know how to do a tattoo, but she wanted my name tattooing on her bum and I didn't know how to do it; so I burned it on with a hot knife. It wasn't life threatening; it wasn't anything, it was done for love. She loved me. She wanted me to give her – put my name on her body ... between us we hit on this idea of using a hot knife on her bum. (*R* v. *Wilson*, 1997, p. 49)

The previous court found that, following the *Brown* judgment, Wilson could not rely on the defence that his wife had wanted the branding to take place. However, the House of Lords found here that this branding was no different to tattooing which is an injury that can be consented to. Moreover:

> Mrs. Wilson not only consented to that which the appellant did, she instigated it. There was no aggressive intent on the part of the appellant. On the contrary, far from wishing to cause injury to his wife, the appellant's desire was to assist her in what she regarded as the acquisition of a desirable piece of personal adornment. (*R* v. *Wilson*, 1997, p. 47)

Concluding their comments, the judges explain that:

> it is not in the public interest that activities such as the appellant's in this appeal should amount to criminal behaviour. Consensual activity between husband and wife, in the privacy of the matrimonial home, is not, in our judgment, normally a proper matter for criminal investigation, let alone criminal prosecution. (*R* v. *Wilson*, 1997, p. 50)

One reading of this judgment might be said to recognise Mrs Wilson's sexual agency. Indeed, her victim status is utterly denied in the judgment. She is referred to as a 'so-called' victim (*R* v. *Wilson*, 1997, p. 48). Her husband is passive in the face of her desires (Houlihan, 2011, p. 50). She wants to be branded by her husband. It is her right to choose what to do with her body. It is not in the public interest for the courts to *intervene* in the affairs of 'consensual activity between husband and wife' or the 'privacy' of the matrimonial home.

Comparing this case to that of *Brown*, as Annette Houlihan (2011) notes, reveals even more of the prejudice that has underpinned the way that

BDSM and BDSM-adjacent activities have been treated in court. In both *Brown* and *Wilson*, activities take place within the context of a desired sexual encounter. In *Wilson*, medical attention was needed. In *Brown*, it was not. In *Wilson*, the injury sustained – though consented to – was permanent. In *Brown*, the injuries sustained were not. In *Brown*, the judges were very worried about the risk of injury, infection and harm that could result from a careless cut or abrasion. In *Wilson*, they were not. A salient difference is that the activities in *Brown* were discursively unable to take place within a matrimonial home because they occurred as part of a group sexual encounter, and not, as we learn in *Wilson*, in the proper place: between husband and wife (see Rubin, 2002 [1984]). The heterosexism of these contrasts does not need to be laboured.

Even though we are told that the defendants in *Brown* were 'sometimes branded' (*R* v. *Brown*, 1993, p. 7), that case appears to be distinguished from *Wilson* in the judgment because the BDSM that appellants in *Brown* engaged in was framed as 'sado-masochism of the grossest kind, involving *inter alia*, physical torture' (*R* v. *Brown*, 1993, p. 50). What happened in *Brown* was sadomasochism, what is happening in *Wilson* is not sadomasochism. It is no 'more dangerous or painful than tattooing' (*R* v. *Wilson*, 1997, p. 50). Thus, saved from being a BDSM or BDSM-adjacent activity, Mrs Wilson *can* consent; even demand it. This analysis relies, as Hoople (1996) might agree, on a stereotyping of what BDSM is, and what it is not. It does not attend to the very eroticised and powerfully charged dynamics that resonate with BDSM-adjacent practices that come with a discussion between a couple about one marking his name upon another. Not going to a professional tattooist but asking her to mark her skin himself evokes the play with power that so much BDSM activity elicits. The submission to the act, even the masochism of the desire to be marked by her husband, brims with BDSM energy. And so, in a somewhat circular fashion, the court decides that this is not BDSM because it is not BDSM. It does not carry the barbaric hallmarks of BDSM; it occurs between husband and wife; therefore, it is 'good'. This case muddies how we might understand consent in these cases, and we should be suspicious of it being a straightforward victory for sexual agency and the recognition of minority sexual rights. Though it looks like Mrs Wilson's right to sexual autonomy is acknowledged, oddly, by sequestering the desire for branding from the practice of BDSM, as Herring notes, the case might also reflect a wilful looking away from intimate partner violence with 'all the hallmarks of coercive control' (2023, p. 40).

A similar tension is evidenced in the case of *R* v. *Slingsby* (1995). Here, Slingsby and his partner were engaged in what we are told was consensual anal and vaginal fisting. Slingsby, wearing a signet ring, injured the victim internally. She developed septicaemia from her injuries and died. He had been convicted of manslaughter in the Crown court, and on appeal, had his conviction quashed because, the judge held, there was no intention to injury. The act of penetrating someone with fingers is not in itself an unlawful act or an assault, where there is consent. The injuries that Slingsby's partner died from were not anticipated by the pair and were not sought out as an end in themselves. Not a sadomasochistic act then, this fisting was 'sex', and where there is consent to sexual practice, there is no assault (Houlihan, 2011, p. 53). In contrast to *Brown*, where no permanent injury was sustained by any of the participants, the death of Slingsby's partner becomes an acceptable risk because it takes place within the confines of what can be recognised, heteronormatively, as sex. The regulation of non-normative sexual practice – especially when it takes place outside of Rubin's charmed centre, in a group, in public space sometimes, between same sex individuals, and using implements – becomes clearer.

A final case to consider within this exploration of the legal landscape in England and Wales is that of *R* v. *Emmett* (1999). Here, as with *Wilson*, the injuries sustained by the victim were reported to the police by the medical practitioner who attended to her. On one occasion Emmett covered his partner's head with a plastic bag whilst he performed oral sex on her. We are told that 'his excitement was such that he had lost track of what was happening to the complainant' (*R* v. *Emmett*, 1999, p. 2) he did not notice that she was in distress and could not breathe. He removed the bag. His partner suffered haemorrhaging in both eyes and bruising on her neck. She sought medical help for these injuries. On another occasion, again, as part of a sex game between the pair, 'lighter fuel was used, and the appellant poured some on to his partner's breasts and set light to it' (*R* v. *Emmett* 1999, p. 3). Emmett's partner sustained a small burn, that at his behest she sought medical help for. The burn was not as serious as Emmett feared and healed completely and without scarring. In their judgments, the court considered the case of *Brown* and of *Wilson* as precedents and held that *Wilson* was different because the 'the actual or potential damage to which the appellant's partner was exposed in this case, plainly went far beyond that which was established by the evidence in *Wilson*' (*R* v. *Emmett*, 1999, p. 6). The injury and risk of injury was too great and so,

> once the conduct of the accused person has gone beyond the permitted limit, however that is defined, in inflicting injury upon or exposing to potential risk his or her partner, in the course of sadomasochistic games whether homo- or heterosexual … he or she *prima facie* at least has committed an offence of a sufficient degree of seriousness

to be convicted of an offence against the person. *Emmett* confirms the law as it was set out in *Brown*. It distinguishes between 'sex' and 'sadomasochism' and contains BDSM within a legal space where it is unconsentable to when the injury sustained is more than 'transient' or 'trifling'.

In 1994, alongside these latter judgments, the Law Commission published a consultation paper entitled 'Consent and Offences against the Person no. 134' which sought to modernise the Offences Against the Person Act 1861 and to address the complexities of consent which were raised by the *Brown* case and numerous critical commentators of that judgment (Giles, 1994; Mullender, 1993). The Law Commission posited that there should be 'no offence for consensual injury of a degree less than the pre-determined limit, or if the harm is in a special category', such as ear piercing, tattooing, or religious flagellation (Ormerod, 1994, pp. 930–1). No definition of what constitutes a 'pre-determined limit' or 'serious injury' is given. The proposals to allow a defence of consent to acts which cause more harm or more injury than currently permitted by the *Brown* judgment were not adopted, though commentary by the Law Commission stated that there were activities 'which, if carried through with the consent of the victim no criminal law system would wish to punish' (Law Commission, 1994, p. 40). Changing the status of the ruling in *Brown* was considered to be a desirable outcome in the Law Commission's recommendations.

These points of law set out the legal terrain as it has stood in England and Wales for decades. Yet, as we started to uncover in Chapter 1, there has been an increase in cases which are far less high profile than the ones addressed here, which mobilise, as part of the defence strategy, the suggestion that injury, or indeed death, that occurs during a sexual encounter occurs because participants have consented to acts which have caused that injury. The *Broadhurst* case that we started with marks a watershed moment for these cases. Following political and activist campaigns about that case, the Domestic Abuse Act 2021 was passed which once more confirmed the law as it is established in *Brown*. S71 provides that 'consent to serious harm for sexual gratification [is] not a defence'.

BDSM IN NORTH AMERICA

In the USA and Canada, legal considerations regarding the legality of criminalisation of BDSM have evolved differently, but hold a similar justice outcome, for now.

In Canada, laws which criminalise BDSM are drawn from a range of legal instruments and case law. Indeed, though not binding in Canada, the judgment in *Brown* is cited as thematically relevant in their consideration of consent, bodily harms and harms to society (Hoople, 1996; e.g. *R* v. *JA*). As Ummi Khan demonstrates, many of the cases which set out the legal framing of consent are not BDSM cases. The case of *Jobibon* concerns a fist fight between two men which resulted in the death of one of the brawlers. The court considered how far consent to participating in a fist fight could be permissible. Whilst consent may be a defence to 'rough sporting activities, medical treatment … and daredevil activities performed by stuntmen' this did not extend to sexual encounters (*R* v. *Welch*, 1995, p. 87). It held that when there was a risk of 'hurt or non-trivial bodily harm' consent was no defence. Indeed, the risk to society of not imposing this limit is framed as potentially 'loosen[ing] the actor's inhibitions against sadism in general' (cited in Khan, 2014, p. 247). Once more, the possibility that BDSM might be pleasurable is held as an expression of 'frail and unstable mental health' and a threat to society itself. Sexual pleasure is insufficiently convincing as a socially valuable cultural product (*R* v. *Welch*, 1995; see also Franke, 2001; Kaplan, 2014). The case of Welch does concern an alleged BDSM encounter between a male and female in which the woman was restrained, beaten and penetrated in the vagina and rectum. He said she consented – asked for and encouraged it – whilst she said it was without her consent. The court agreed that what took place was against her consent but that even if it had not been:

> when the activity in question involves pursuing sexual gratification by deliberately inflicting pain upon another that gives rise to bodily harm, then the personal interest of the individuals involved must yield to the more compelling societal interests which are challenged by such behaviour. (*R* v. *Welch*, 1995, p. 88)

Non-normative sexual desire is once again incompatible with social good. These observations mean that intentional BDSM – which is known to have the potential to cause some harm – is unlikely to be able to be consented to in law.

R v. *JA* (2011) is another Canadian case that has received a significant amount of legal scrutiny (Gotell, 2012; Busby, 2012; Khan, 2016b). This case concerns a male and female long-term couple who had a practice of engaging in BDSM sexual practice, including edgeplay involving erotic asphyxiation. During one of their encounters, the female complainant was choked to unconsciousness. During this time, her male partner tied her hands up and inserted a dildo into her anus. When she regained consciousness, the penetration continued for a short period. She safe-worded; he cut her restraints. Several weeks later she reported the incident to the police; 'while she consented to the choking, she had not consented to the sexual activity that had occurred' (*R* v. *JA*, 2011, p. 4). JA was charged with sexual assault and aggravated assault. JA's partner recanted her complaint and testified that she consented to everything that they did together and that she had only made a complaint because JA had threatened to take sole custody of their son. In this case, the Supreme Court held that:

> The jurisprudence has consistently interpreted consent as requiring a conscious, operating mind, capable of granting, revoking or withholding consent to each and every sexual act. The jurisprudence also establishes that there is no substitute for the complainant's actual consent to the sexual activity at the time it occurred. It is not sufficient for the accused to have believed the complainant was consenting: he must also take reasonable steps to ascertain consent and must believe that the complainant communicated her consent to engage in the sexual activity in question. This is impossible if the complainant is unconscious … When the complainant loses consciousness, she loses the ability to either oppose or consent to the sexual activity that occurs. (*R* v. *JA*, 2011, p. 5)

Khan (2014, pp. 256–7) notes here how once again, BDSM practice, safe-wording and anal penetration are all figured in excessive, pathologised terms. The judgment states that what JA's partner experienced was dehumanising and degrading, notwithstanding her own agentic claims to the contrary in court. The impossibility of consent, the construction of BDSM desire as pathology, and the specific erasure of masochistic desire, all emerge on this Canadian landscape (Khan, 2014), and sadomasochistic desire becomes, itself, a signifier of dangerousness and risk to social life.

In the USA, the legal landscape is forged differently from that in Canada and England and Wales, and this is in part due to the incremental state-by-state development of criminal law. Over the past few hundred years, each of the fifty states of the USA has developed its own criminal code. Though similarities exist across the states, it is not possible to succinctly point to 'the' US law on BDSM, or any other non-federal crime. Similarities which do exist emerge thanks to the widespread, but not universal, adoption of the Model Penal Code (MPC), which is the closest things get in the USA to an American Criminal Code (Robinson & Dubber, 2007). Discerning the legal landscape in the USA is trickier then, but there are some key cases which help to build this picture.

The case of *People* v. *Samuels* takes us to California in 1967 – two years before the Stonewall riots and the flourishing of the LGBT movement in the USA – and the sending of a film depicting Martin Samuels's sadomasochistic acts which included whipping and restraints with a consenting, but unknown, submissive male partner. The film was deemed obscene. Samuels tried to raise a defence of consent on the part of the man in his film to refute the assault charges that he faced. In the commentary, the court states that 'it is a matter of common knowledge that a normal person in possession of his mental faculties does not freely consent to the use, upon himself, of force likely to produce great bodily injury' (cited in Ridinger, 2006, p. 198). Samuels's assault conviction was upheld despite there being no identifiable victim and no complaining witness.

In 1980, the case of *Commonwealth* v. *Appleby* was tried in Massachusetts. This also concerned two men who lived together in what was described as a master–servant relationship. The physical aggression meted out to the submissive partner over time became more extreme. The submissive partner eventually left the relationship, saying that he was living in fear, had low self-esteem and felt trapped by Appleby. The judgment in this case placed SM behaviour into the same category as that for victims of intimate partner violence (Ridinger, 2006). It confirmed that as a matter of public policy, it should not be possible for someone to consent to assault within a sexual context. Arguably, what happened in this case may have been a BDSM relationship which became abusive. Certainly, practitioners of BDSM may not recognise the dynamic described by Appleby's victim as one in which meaningful consent had been given to this master–servant relationship.

Lawrence v. *Texas* (2003) is a landmark case in the evolution of sexual rights in the USA as it holds that it is illegal to criminalise private consensual sex between men and effectively outlawed anti-sodomy laws. The case has been interpreted to 'declare unconstitutional any legislation that is motivated solely by moral concerns' (Haley, 2015, p. 637) and, whilst this is not a case about BDSM, it is about sexual citizenship rights. In Nebraska, however, in the case of *State* v. *Van*, the court confirmed that privacy rights protected under *Lawrence* do not extend to BDSM, but only to 'conduct that does not cause injury' to others (Haley, 2015, p. 637). Commentators note that morally motivated law-making – such as that addressed in *Lawrence* – is unconstitutional (Onoma, 2017) and that the continuing criminalisation of BDSM is a social and legal injustice (Haley 2015; Pa, 2001).

Consent within BDSM is more closely examined in the case of *People* v. *Jovanovic* (1999). Here, a male and female college student met online and, through emails, discussed a mutual interest in BDSM. The exchanges detailed what they wanted to do together, including using hot wax, anal penetration, binding, biting and blindfolding. When they met, the complainant stated that Jovanovic ignored her wishes to stop, ignored her safe word and kept her from leaving his apartment for twenty hours. Jovanovic was found guilty of kidnapping, sexual abuse and assault. He was sentenced to fifteen years in prison. He served five years in prison before his case was overturned on appeal because it was held that the emails sent between the pair prior to this meeting should have been included as evidence for the defence to show that what took place between them was something that the complainant had expressed an interest in, and potentially was evidence of her consent. Though this looks like it could be a sign that the court in New York was prepared to recognise a defence of consent to BDSM, the court insist that that 'there is no defence of consent on a change of assault' (*People* v. *Jovanovic*, 1999, p. 197).

So far, the fact of consent as a possible defence to BDSM practice has been skirted by the courts. However, in 2021, following years of activism from the National Coalition for Sexual Freedom (NCSF) amongst others, the MPC was amended to include section 213.10: the 'affirmative defence of explicit prior permission'. This amendment offers the legal possibility for people to consent to being threatened, having physical force or restraint used on them, having their absence of consent ignored as long as permission for this is given prior to engaging in sexual conduct. The MPC states in sections 213.10.2 that permission is only explicit when given orally or in writing, it must specify when unwillingness to continue can be ignored; what specific forms of force restraint will take place, using what, how long for; and what the safe words will be. Some exceptions to this include the age requirement that parties are over eighteen (which is interesting, considering that the age of consent in many states is sixteen or seventeen); the conduct must not cause or risk serious injury; and the person consenting must not be incapacitated or otherwise vulnerable. Conduct must be sexual and must include oral sex, penetration, intimate touching for the purposes of arousing or gratifying sexual pleasure. The NCSF found that 90 per cent of BDSM practitioners defined their practice as sexual. Though, as Burch and Salmon (2019) also demonstrate, not everyone who does engage in BDSM will recognise their practice as sexual in this way. This means that whilst a considerable amount of BDSM will be 'consentable to', edgeplay, including breath play, will not be covered by this explicit permission provision. Likewise, nor will conduct which is not sexual.

The MPC is drafted by the American Legal Institution and is intended to inform law across the USA. Until the MPC guidelines are accommodated into all state laws, capacity for consent to BDSM will remain patchy, but the MPC is authoritative. It also marks a departure from a criminalisation trend across different jurisdictions. Drafted in consultation with activist groups, it reflects how BDSM practitioners actually do consent negotiations in ideal circumstances (Dunkley & Brotto, 2020), with safeguards, negotiations and the setting of limits. As Anna Onoma (2017) notes, recognising that BDSM practice exists, and can exist ethically, is a stepping stone towards destigmatising BDSM. This enhances understanding of the subculture, encourages victims of consent violations within BDSM practice to come forward and, as Theodore Bennett (2021) also demonstrates, by bringing BDSM practice out into the light, it makes it harder for perpetrators of intimate partner violence or BDSM-adjacent activity to present what they have done as rough sex that has 'gone wrong'.

'SEX WARS'

Debates about how to approach BDSM from a feminist, justice-orientated perspective have abounded for decades and, indeed, continue to proliferate. As Carol Vance (1993, p. 295) notes in her reflections on the Barnard sexuality conference which was widely held to mark one of the turning points of contemporary feminism, it was 'sado-masochism, pornography, and butch-femme roles among lesbians' that became a synecdoche for contemporary sexual crises. These so-called 'sex wars' came to dominate discourses about how best to 'do' feminist work and how to approach feminist concerns about sexual justice, sexual agency, anti-violence and freedom.

Of these, BDSM, and more vehemently, pornography (possibly because the butch-femme issue is of little interest to a heteronormative legislative majority), became issues that were adopted by moral conservatives and fundamentalists to draft bills and ordinances that would criminalise certain publications and enshrine, 'witting or unwittingly', the feminist alliance with 'moral conservatives who in many other – anti-gay, anti-birth-control, anti-abortion – ways, did not have feminist preoccupations at all' (Vance, 1984, pp. 303–5). This rift set up a narrative, which Lorna Bracewell (2021, p. 5) calls the 'catfight narrative'; the idea that on the one hand anti-sex/sex-negative/anti-porn/pro-censorship feminist activism was pitted against pro-sex/sex-positive/anti-censorship/sexual liberal feminism on the other, and that there were no points of connection.

Against this background, where we are asked to agree that positions are polarised and intransigent, it is not surprising that careful thought about how to make feminist politics work for everyone has been stifled, and why imagination about how to create new ways of living in a socially and sexually just world, atrophy. In fact, as we see in the context of debates about BDSM from this time, and in the current climate, conflict about the proper status of BDSM practice and desire, here from a socio-legal perspective, can be more nuanced, and curious, about the differences between them.

Contemporary debates that endure about what to do with the BDSM problem can be understood as a continuation, albeit under a different guise, of these 'sex war' dynamics. Visceral corollaries are found in trans and gender critical discourse, and sex work/sex trafficking activism. Many scholars are critical of the continued criminalisation of BDSM (Pa, 2001; Califia, 1981 [1980]; Khan, 2020; Haley, 2015). Monica Pa (2001, p. 71) argues that the way that BDSM is treated by the law is an expression of 'intolerance for sexual difference'. The right to practice BDSM without legal penalty should be afforded BDSM practitioners in recognition of their sexual agency and capacity to choose to do it, she argues. We saw in the judgment in *Brown* that BDSM is figured as dangerous and 'uncivil' because it is considered to be so unthinkingly dangerous, so incomprehensible, that it must be curtailed for the public good. Pleasure derived from pain is 'an evil thing' (*R* v. *Brown*, 1993, p. 9). Pleasure is not enough (Kaplan, 2014).

Judgments which uncritically align BDSM with violence fail to take into consideration the full complexity of a practice which has a nuanced approach to consent, desire and power play (Pa, 2001, p. 76). Sequestering BDSM practice from 'sex', as we have seen in the cases above, figures BDSM as assault which cannot be consented to. This form of sexual exceptionalism, where practices are treated differently because they are 'sex', is the avenue that Pa mobilises to argue for a defence of consent to be available in BDSM cases. Figured as sex, BDSM can then 'be consented to' in the same way that other sex can be consented to.

For Daniel Haley (2015), creating a consent defence for BDSM practice is the right thing to do because moral imperatives have no place (or ought to have no place) in legal decision-making. Yet, if we think of sex as 'exceptional', this too is a moral position. Haley (2015, p. 640) posits that the law states that 'individuals have a liberty right'; to conduct their intimate relationships 'free from government intrusion'. In short, to deny this defence is to 'deny [the BDSM practitioner] the right to love' (2015, p. 641) – a denial as intrinsically egregious as the historical criminalisation of homosexuality. These discriminatory regimes are sex negative, moralistic, and impinge on the liberty rights which are apparently the bastions of contemporary society in the post industrialised global north where these cases have played out (Cowan, 2010, p. 8; Khan, 2016a).

In these interactions, creating a consent defence is a necessary imperative because it destigmatises BDSM practice. It encourages the BDSM-curious to learn more about the subculture; to attend workshops, to read literature, to discuss techniques with peers – all practices that are common in the BDSM subculture – to better understand BDSM practice. A better-informed BDSM practitioner is also one less likely to harm their partner(s). Removing prohibitions around BDSM practice encourages reporting of abuse where it does occur. Eliminating criminal prosecution where both partners agree that activities were consensual makes for a better exercise of the law. There is sexism, ableism and homophobia in the way that BDSM is treated in court. Legal protection for BDSM practice would start the work of diminishing that, by creating a pathway for enhanced social and sexual justice (see Pa, 2001; Haley, 2015).

For some scholars, such a proposition is problematic (Hanna, 2001). It is the state's obligation to its citizenry to curtail violence. Indeed, the right to exercise violence must remain in the hands of the state, so that it alone may sanction between legitimate and illegitimate violence. Curtailing all other violence is a public good, and 'the social goals of promoting human dignity are better served by limiting, not extending the doctrine of violent consent' (2001, p. 248). For this reason, there should be no consent defence available in BDSM cases. The imperative for sexual autonomy is outweighed by a public interest need to protect society from violence. For Hanna (2001, p. 256), a consent defence could be used to justify male sexual violence, providing an alibi for abusive behaviour. Pa (2001, p. 86) deals with this by highlighting that this potential for abuse occurs wherever consent defences exist – notably in cases of sexual assault and rape. Solutions, for Pa, include better education about what BDSM is, and what it is not. Indeed, as noted above, many BDSM scholars have provided insights which inform the distinction between abuse and consensual BDSM (Moser & Madeson, 1998; Dunkley & Brotto, 2020; Jozifkova, 2013; Pitagora, 2013). Beyond those guidelines, Haley (2015, p. 645) suggests that if, within a consent defence, the burden of proof on the defendant was high, if they had to positively show that consent was present, perhaps through evidence of 'emails and texts discussing desire to participate in BDSM activities', only then might such a defence become available to a defendant. Yet, for Herring (2023) and for Joseph Fischel (2019) the problem of a 'consent defence' poses a symbolic, societal problem.

The mainstreaming of BDSM practice occurs against a background of increased sexualisation in society; there is the expectation that people will *want* to play sex games and do rough sex (Herring, 2023, p. 45). This hyper-sexualisation assumes that sex is always 'good' and is another form of sexual exceptionalism, where 'kinky' sex is expected. This happens – within a heteronormative encounter – along a gendered dynamic where women are dominated by men (indeed, each of the cases that I address in this text are like this) and where this domination is normalised, expected and desired (see Gavey, 2024). Following Catherine MacKinnon, Herring suggests that BDSM rehearses 'rape myths that "women say no when they mean yes"', and 'women will "consent" if some pressure is used' (2023, p. 46). This symbolic and societal harm is too important to let slide behind a consent defence.

Moreover, regardless of what practitioners of BDSM say that they are doing when they are conducting a master/slave, Nazi/Jew, priest/nun, cop/suspect or Abu Ghraib torture scene (Califia, 1981 [1980]; Weiss, 2009), what they are actually doing is 'expropriating' the experiences of oppressed people for their own pleasure (Hawthorne, 2006 cited in Herring, 2023, p. 47). This culturally reinforces sexual violence, and it endorses oppression of minoritised people. It simply is too close to – too cognate with – violence against women and girls to be pardoned (Herring, 2023, p. 47). Likewise, for Fischel, BDSM has the capacity to interfere too much with human flourishing and dignity. Moreover, though it is the posterchild of 'good' BDSM, consent, as we shall see, is not even the best measure of making sure that what happens within a sexual encounter promotes sexual justice or, in Fischel's (2019, p. 3) words, nurtures a 'democratically hedonic sexual culture'.

Thus, we can see on the one hand, a call for BDSM to be protected from prosecution because it respects individual liberties: it recognises sexually minoritised positionalities and acknowledges practitioners' sexual autonomy and 'freedom to choose'. On the other hand, objections about permitting a BDSM defence are equally political; the relationship to gendered violence is too proximate, the symbolism of the harm too great, and these concerns are not taken seriously enough by the BDSM activists who call for these changes in the first place.

Finding ourselves at this impasse within this sexual landscape, I want to explore how to operate within this tension, to potentially navigate a way through it.

THE FEMINIST PROBLEM

How to think our way through this impasse? As a starting point (or maybe the end of the starting point) Janet Halley suggests that we consider 'taking a break from feminism'. Analysing a Texan divorce proceeding from 1990 in which the wife sues her former husband for emotional distress sustained because her husband convinced her to try BDSM activity which triggered for her a traumatic memory of being raped at knife point when she was younger, Janet Halley (in Cossman et al. 2003, pp. 611–13) suggests that a feminist reading of this posits women as always in relation to men, and always-already in a relation of subservience and victimhood. From this forever-victim positionality, women can never be agent and can only suffer in sexual encounters with men. Sheila, the wife, is always-already rape victim and becomes, in her claim against the husband, defined in some essential way by this status. Once more exemplifying the knots that we can tie ourselves up with when we rely on consent discourses, Sheila's consent to try BDSM for her husband's pleasure becomes coercion, and rape becomes unrecoverable from. Moreover, the BDSM practice which condemns the husband relies on a form of 'governance' feminism and a pro-carceral ethic which fosters intersectional violence and colludes with masculinist institutions of juridical power.

For these reasons, Halley suggests that to interrogate justice outcomes in cases like these, we would do better to leave feminism alone. Feminism, Halley suggests, does not help here. Though Halley offers alternatives tools with which to understand this impasse, my question is how much of a problem is feminism here? And if feminism is a problem, why is this so?

Califia (1981 [1980]) and Marie France (1984) both separately explore the tensions between feminism and sadomasochism. Both papers are over forty years old, but they both still work first, to illuminate the terrain of debates about deviant sexuality which are central to reading this sexual landscape, and second, to remind us that the contested views we continue to grapple with are not new, but rather are echoes of ongoing trouble. Califia's (1981 [1980]) paper 'Feminism and Sadomasochism' is a deeply personal rage against prejudice towards lesbian sadomasochists meted out by elements of the feminist movement, and the lesbian feminist movement more specifically. France's (1984) 'Sadomasochism and Feminism' acts as an indirect response to Califia and appeals to an analysis of BDSM beyond the 'essential' identitarian politics which appear in some pro-BDSM arguments: 'we're perverted but we like it' (France, 1984, p. 36). France (1984, p. 35) calls for BDSM to be 'better defended as one of a multitude of bodily possibilities' for sexual practice and offers, instead, an analysis of BDSM politics through Freudian and Foucaultian analytical lenses. So maybe she is taking a break from feminism too.

Though Califia appears, at some level, to be attached to feminist principles – seeking a 'rapprochement' between BDSM and feminism – he is clear here too, that sadomasochists need to take a break from feminism as a movement in which they 'do not do their homework' about BDSM and wilfully misread it as abuse. France (1984, p. 35) wonders whether, rather than being uninformed about BDSM, its critics see it as a practice that might 'ape' patriarchal sexual relations rather than resist them, as Califia posits: BDSM is not as politically potent as it thinks it is. However, as Califia also states, BDSM is about more than the genitals. It is eroticism that calls on the whole body as a site of sensation. It challenges heteronormative sex, androcentric desire, the tyranny of romantic love. Yet, even with all this potentiality, notes France (1984, p. 38), this reading of BDSM as inherently resistant works to romanticise the body and sex itself, as the pinnacle of what can be achieved in a human life, as something 'bigger, better and brighter' than any other form of sexual encounter.

Reducing discourses about sexual practice as something that is essentially good or bad or freeing or oppressive is, as I will argue, one of the problems with contemporary debates about BDSM in particular, and anxiety about sex more broadly. As Halley notes, by aligning with conservative sexual mores, BDSM critics who root their complaint in feminist activism get into bed with the same politics that was/is instrumental in denigrating and subordinating women elsewhere. Both of these feminism/sadomasochism papers seem to need to take their distance from feminist politics and yet, for Califia (1981 [1980], pp. 169–70) at least, feminism remains vital because it is one of the only politics (we can also add queer approaches) which contests the patriarchy which 'prevents women from becoming complete and independent human beings'.

Though we see that Halley's alternative Nietzschean and Foucaultian analyses of the Texan divorce case give us different perspectives on what is at stake there, we could argue that the feminism which Halley suggests casts Sheila as always-already victim is really a purist (or puritanical) theory of feminism and perhaps an idealist misreading of the work that feminism does. Yes, of course, feminism, as it is figured by Halley, renders Sheila the victim of heteropatriarchy and erodes any potentiality of her agency, but it is also feminism that helps Sheila to name her suffering as one rooted in trauma of a historical rape. Feminist activism has aided to criminalise marital rape, so that it is not merely part and parcel of what women are expected to submit to within marriage, but recognised as a wrong in itself. Feminism also recognises the demonisation of the BDSM-desiring man – in this case – being made to pay for his perversions.

Halley herself (in Cossman et al. 2003, p. 606) acknowledges that feminisms can be hybrid and cut along intersectional lines of identity (e.g. post-colonial feminism, socialist feminism). Of course feminism must be about gender and sexuality and not simply only women if it is to have purchase (Califia, 1981 [1980]). We can add to this the importance of queer approaches as tools which help us to challenge dominant power narratives – the dominance of heteronormativity, of cis-genderism, of Anglocentrism – and to embrace different potentialities in the expression of sexual desire. It is here that Califia's call against patriarchy resonates. Patriarchy is bad for everybody. People suffer through patriarchy in different ways and to different extents, depending on their sex, age, disability, attractiveness, whiteness, wealth, sexuality and so on. Very few men experience patriarchy as an unqualified benefit. Queer and feminist approaches help us to see this and to analyse the taken for granted of sexuality and gender matters – particularly in legal contexts – in order to strive for gendered social justice. Or what Califia calls 'becoming complete'. Or, in the words of Fischel, living a 'democratically hedonic life'.

NEGATIVE POSITIVITY

Whether we are taking a break from feminism or not, what is clear is that debates on either side of the sadomasochistic argument are rooted in distinct(ly) feminist traditions. These traditions are usually figured as being defined through their relationship with sex positivity and negativity. Within criminology and socio-legal studies, there are ever-increasing calls for a turn towards a sex positive criminal justice system (Wodda & Panfil, 2020). Many will be familiar with the principles espoused through sex positive and sex negative politics.

Sex negativity posits that sex is 'inherently bad' (Glickman, 2000, p. 1). Sex negativity has been described as an approach to sexual practice which is moralistic – sex is a problem – and sexually minoritised practices such as homosexuality or sadomasochism are deviant, dangerous or criminal. Sex negativity is punitive. It is discriminatory. The intransigence of sex negativity fosters prejudice and exclusion that is aligned with sexism, racism, transphobia, homophobia, ageism, ableism and so on (Williams et al., 2013; Glickman, 2000). Only certain bodies are allowed to fuck in a sex negative world. And when they are, they are only allowed to do so in specific 'charmed' ways (Rubin, 2002 [1984]). Acceptable sexual practices take place within the confines of a marriage or committed relationship, procreative sex is preferred, sex should involve only one other person (no more, no less). Pornography, sex work, masturbation, promiscuity, non-normative sexual practice, indeed sexual desire itself are condemned through sex negative approaches.

Often offered as sex negativity's opposite, sex positivity normalises sex in all its abundance (Glickman, 2000). Sex positivity, for the purposes of this book, recognises pleasure, desire and sexual diversity as normative (Williams et al., 2013). Sex positivity is accepting of difference, respectful of individual choices around sex (including the choice not to have sex), and harbours the potentiality to offer an approach to sex outside of patriarchal and heteronormative strictures (Ivanski & Kohut, 2017). Sex positivity does not posit that all sex is good or that sex is compulsory, but rather that through sex positivity we can free ourselves from the confines of sexual sanctions (Rubin, 2002 [1984]; Williams et al., 2013; Glickman, 2000). Sex positivity is epistemologically pro-gender equality, anti-racist, anti-ableist, pro-queer, and can be mobilised to counter the discrimination that sex negativity enforces elsewhere.

Critics of sex positivity suggest that one of the limitations of a pro-sex approach is that it is apolitical. It does not attend to the circumstances in which specific sexual practices or desires are demonised and others valorised (Glick, 2000). Indeed, as Bracewell (2021) notes in the context of #MeToo, the backlash against a movement committed to giving voice to experiences of sexual violence connects sexual conservatives concerned about so-called 'mob justice' with what she calls 'sex positive' feminist bemoaning that flirtations have now become demonised. Sex positivity here becomes framed as something which silences oppression, which invites victims of sexual violence to 'just get on with it'. Sexual variation, the validation of diversity and sexual difference has also fostered the commodification of open-mindedness through the sexualisation of contemporary culture, the increased availability of pornography and the normalisation of representations of sexual violence

(Ivanski & Kohut, 2017). All of these instances show some of the complexity of appeals to the sex positive *tout court*, without attending to the conditions in which that positivity emerges. Sex positivity can, indeed, be spectacularised. Like consent, it can be offered as a magic bullet which might fix the troubles that sexuality causes. Negative positivity – holding space for sex positivity to be in tension with what it can do – is a way to embrace the potentialities of the sex positivity and troubling it when it becomes spectacularised, or compulsory.

Debates around sadomasochism are often also figured as being in oppositional positions in these different camps. Desire for sadomasochism is cast as a social construction, a reiteration of patriarchal power relations and an internalisation of heterosexism on the one hand, and on the other, the demonisation of sadomasochism denies the sexual agency of SM practitioners, curtails their sexual citizenship rights, and becomes aligned with the moral conservatism (Linden et al., 1982; Califia 1981 [1980], Rubin, 2002 [1984]; Hopkins, 1994; Srinivasan, 2021). Yet, as our queerer approaches help us to see, that distinction, though tidy, is not one that we can let this analysis get away with.

It is clear to me, with the contemporary state of things, that we emerge as more fully blooming sexual citizens in a context where sexuality and sexual diversity is something that we can address without shame. Being able to name what we like, what we don't like, what we feel, what we fear and to be able to do that without fear of ridicule, or diminishment, is part of what helps us to live 'complete' sexual lives (Califia, 1981 [1980]). To be able to recognise sexual harms by naming them and helping others to name them fosters sexual and social justice. Sex positive principles within sex education, for instance, acknowledges sexual diversity, normalised difference, and has the capacity to equip people with insights that they need to make meaningful decisions about their sexual practices. It helps them to recognise their desires. For Williams et al. (2013) these emancipatory approaches help to combat discrimination and reduce sexual offending. These are principles that it is hard to take issue with.

Yet, it is also clear, as Amia Srinivasan's (2021) discussion of pornography demonstrates, that permissiveness and hyper accessibility of porn and the sexualisation of culture does also foster circumstances which entrench sexist, misogynistic, heteropatriarchal politics, where sexual availability and adventure is normative. And this does risk, as Elisa Glick (2000) warns us, that we do not sufficiently engage in the socio-cultural conditions of our sex as more and more of it becomes more and more available.

Twenty-five years ago, in a pre-internet era, in the small town in which I lived, if I wanted to buy a vibrator or other sex toy, such an acquisition could usually only be made in disconcerting-looking stores with blacked out windows with ambiguous names about being 'private' or 'adult'. Now, I can by a bullet vibrator in the same supermarket aisle where I pick up my multivitamins. A cause for celebration perhaps, as masturbation and non-penetrative, non-phallocentric sex becomes more normalised? Similarly, twenty-five years ago, if I wanted to send a sexy image to my partner and did not have access to a polaroid camera and film, I would have had to take the picture using a conventional camera, loading it with film, take it to be processed when the film was full, and, after waiting for the printing to be complete, post, or give my sexy image to my partner. The process seems quaint when compared to the instantaneous way that I could now send sexy images using my phone. Indeed, sexting in this way can be considered to be becoming a normative part of dating and maintaining a relationship (Van Ouytsel et al., 2020). Destigmatising the sending of sexual images in this way frees people to express their sexual desire or their sexual selves. But it is also associated with bullying and harassment behaviours. Indeed, creating revenge porn, image-based sexual violence, or 'deep fake' sexual images, or even threatening to do so, using sexual images that may have been created consensually, has since been criminalised in England and Wales (Ministry of Justice, 2023).

So, an evolving approach to sexuality, desire and sexual practice in the public domain might resonate with sex positive principles of acceptance and non-judgement, but we can also see that it is not far out of the grips of a gendered violence which evolves and proliferates as much as these more liberatory attitudes to sex appear to emerge. Sex positivity and negativity are more appropriately figured as interwoven dynamics that sculpt the contemporary sexual landscape than as neat adversaries.

Against Sadomasochism (Linden et al., 1982) is a vibrant text whose treatise supports its title. Much of it is what would be described as sex negative in approach. In it, sadomasochistic desire is cast as an expression of 'unacknowledged pain in the self' (Harris, 1982, p. 95). Its legitimation is the preoccupation of dominant groups who are 'not trying to change the system' but who benefit from the subordination of women and ethnic minorities (Lorde & Star, 1982, p. 69). Its focus on the eroticisation of power is the wrong question: the feminist goal is not the expression – or even equalisation of power, but rather the elimination of power dynamics in sexual … relationships (Rian, 1982, p. 49). Pro-sadomasochistic discourse is grounded in Orwellian newspeak – 'freedom-through-bondage, pain-is-pleasure' – the repetition of which 'will more likely cause habituation or addiction' (Meredith, 1982, p. 97). And yet, many of the contributors to the volume are emphatic in their refusal to condemn sadomasochistic practice from a moral perspective:

> I ask myself, under close scrutiny, whether I am puritanical about this ... and the answer is no. I feel that we make integrated life decisions about the networks of our lives ... if they don't lead us towards growth and change, we have nothing to build on, no future. (Lorde & Star, 1982, p. 69)

Thus, it is not the moral repugnance that we see in the *Brown* judgment above that encourages the contributors to this volume to condemn sado-masochism, it is rather that the politics of the practice are not considered to be good enough; they are not radical enough to foster social cultural change. A contingent sex negativity, perhaps.

These radical feminist critiques might be salient to the current question. BDSM is more mainstream, but is it 'better'? Is it the liberatory, emancipating practice that we are told it can be (Califia, 1981 [1980]; Rubin, 2002 [1984]; Cowan 2010)? Or does it remain mired in the intersectional abuses of power, of misogynistic apologia that Ruth Linden et al. (1982) and Ros Walling-Wefelmeyer and Tully O'Neill (2021) warn us of? Intertwining sex positive and negative voices through an analytical plurality – a negative positivity – helps us to perceive these nuances.

SEXUAL EXCEPTIONALISM

> In sex, people experience earlier substrates, irrational connections, infantile memories, and a range of rich sensations. We fear dependency and possible loss of control, as well as our greedy aggressions, our wishes to incorporate body parts, even entire persons. Having been told that pleasure threatens desire, we wonder: what if there is no end to desire? (Vance, 1984, p. 5)

In the opening to *Pleasure and Danger*, Vance captures an important dynamic that is easy to overlook. The libidinal draw of the erotic is in this interplay between what thrills us and what terrifies. The interplay between loss of control, abandon, and feelings of completeness and plenitude captures this sense of being overpowered – penetrated – by the significance of a sexual encounter, whether we want it to or not. It marks sexual practice as a psychic, embodied, socio-cultural, personal and primordial encounter all at once. A singular human (and more-than-human) interaction. It speaks, in part, to why we hold sex to be in some way, exceptional.

The exceptionalism of sex is one of the reasons why it is dealt with so peculiarly by the criminal justice system. 'Sex is not a sport', Cheryl Hanna (2001) reminds us, which is one of the reasons why BDSM practice cannot avail itself of a 'consent defence' in the same way that rough sports can do. Sexual exceptionalism both makes things much worse and much better than if there was no sex. Relationships such as marriages, parenting arrangements and civil partnerships are formally recognised socially and in law and benefit from being desirable, or sanctioned, in a way that different arrangements (polyamory, families of choice, non-romantic non-kinship ties) are not. A presumption exists that sexual practice takes place in these former arrangements; sex that happens in the latter arrangements poses more social problems. Similarly, in England and Wales, sexual assault can be punished more severely (up to ten years in custody) than assaults without a sexual element to them (up to five years in custody) (Sentencing Council, n.d. a, b). At the same time, sex crimes are, in England and Wales, amongst the hardest to secure a conviction for. In 2022/3 only 1.6% of rapes reported to the police ended in a conviction. There are lots of reasons for this, many of which are not in the scope of my analysis in this book, but one of those will be the generalised squeamishness associated with labelling a person a rapist; a far more stigmatised label than 'assaulter', for instance.

Claims for sexual exceptionalism accompany claims for sexual citizenship rights and 'the right to freely express one's sexuality', including the right to be sadomasochistic (Haley, 2015, p. 640). It is sexual exceptionalism that holds that 'a raped woman has suffered an injury from which she is unlikely ever to recover' (Cossman et al., 2003, p. 610). It is sexual exceptionalism that makes any claims to the contrary of this impossible to say. As Gayle Rubin (1984) and Khan (2014) demonstrate, it is sexual exceptionalism that vilifies and denigrates sexual subcultures, including sadomasochistic subcultures, leading to their persecution in law. Conversely, sexual exceptionalism transforms potential abuse into acts that take place in the 'privacy of the matrimonial home' beyond the glare of legal scrutiny. 'Sex sells', 'no means no' and 'consent is sexy' are all expressions of sexual exceptionalism.

Fischel (2019, p. 27) asks, 'why is sex special?'. This is a question that I will come back to in the course of this book. What matters about this question, for now, is that it is special, and that this specialness, this exceptionality, is part of the landscape in which sexual practices become troublesome. Fischel (2019, p. 28) notes that sometimes our thinking 'fuzzes out' when it comes to thinking about sex and consent. This is also an expression of its exceptionalism. Another way of thinking about this is that sex is spectacularised and enchanting. And the ways that it enchants us fosters this fuzzy thinking about sex; obfuscating what is going on when we hold sex to be exceptional.

SPECTACULARISATION AND ENCHANTMENT

Throughout these debates – for, against or ambivalent about sexual expression – run intertwining themes that become relevant for the more specific analysis of cases considered in the rest of this book: the concepts of spectacularisation and (dis)enchantment.

Indeed, the discourses for and against BDSM that I have outlined here, and which echo the so-called sex wars of the 1970/80s, are spectacularised in contemporary debates. The spectacle of the spectacle moves us further and further away from understanding the conditions of contemporary sexual landscapes and further propels contemporary rape culture.

Part of what is afoot in these discussions can be understood as a form of enchantment with consent. The notion of enchantment emerges, perhaps counter-intuitively, in Max Weber's articulation of disenchantment, drawn from Friedrich Schiller's 1788 poem lamenting the 'de-divination of nature' (Green, 2005, p. 54). From this, Weber identifies a secularisation, de-mystification and unmagicking which makes the world more knowable and more impersonal (Jenkins, 2000, p. 12). Disenchantment makes the world more rational, bureaucratic, measurable. It is a bedrock of modernity, predictability and control, towards what George Ritzer describes as the McDonaldization of society; everything is efficient, everything is the same, everything is dehumanising (Ritzer, 1996, pp. 293–4). *Contra* this, scholars suggest that what we actually see is a return to enchantment, or re-enchantment in contemporary society (Sherry, 2009; Jenkins, 2000; Creighton, 2022). If enchantment describes a belief in wonder, magic and myth then modernity is also saturated with magic-like beliefs in science, technology, media to name a few 'new gods' (Jenkins, 2000). As some of the discourses around consent demonstrate, merely stating 'yes means yes' and the 'no means no' becomes an example of magical, enchanted thinking about the power of consent (Fanghanel & Lim, 2017). For Heidi M. Hurd, this is the 'moral magic' of consent which turns an assault into a boxing match, a 'battery into a handshake' (1996, p. 123). Consent becomes an illocutionary act which brings about these transformations. By simply believing that consent is enough, incomplete and unsatisfying conclusions about sexual encounters emerge. Claims that BDSM should be legally permissible because it is consensual hold consent in as much magical suspense as do discourses that support rape myths on the same basis. Becoming enchanted with consent and with sexual desire and practice more broadly sustains contemporary rape culture, all the while cloaking the complexities of consent under a mystical, undifferentiable, unrationalisable guise.

THE CASES

In this chapter, we have examined the ways that BDSM, BDSM-adjacent activity and sexual subcultures interact in a contemporary sexual landscape. This chapter has enabled us to understand diverse legal positions and to appreciate those against the specific backdrop in which they exist. That is, the sexual cultures of much of the global north, with its neoliberal, heteronormative, imperialist and occasionally paternalistic underpinnings. The feminist and queer politics which have also inflected this landscape have also helped us to fathom how we got here, including the potentials and the problems of these politics. From this point, we can dive deeper into understanding the specific phenomenon of how sex that is rough – games that go wrong – are constructed, constituted, and confronted in the courtroom.

First, and finally, let us meet the cases.

R v. *Bailey* (2018): Richard Bailey killed Charlotte Teeling in 2018 by applying pressure to her neck during a consensual sexual encounter. He pleaded not guilty to her murder and said that what happened was an accident. He said he was strangling her at her behest. He was found guilty of murder and sentenced to a minimum term of twenty-nine years in prison.

R v. *Broadhurst* (2018): In 2016 John Broadhurst left his girlfriend Natalie Connolly to die at the bottom of his staircase following a day of heavy drinking and drug taking. The bleeding from internal injuries sustained during their rough sexual encounter, coupled with her intoxication, were the causes of death. He said that she was asking for more ‘extreme’ things to be done to her during sex. He pleaded guilty to manslaughter by gross negligence and was sentenced to three years and eight months imprisonment.

R v. *Coates* (2012): Marcus Coates killed Jennie Banner in 2011. He said that they had tried to have a casual sexual relationship. They took drugs together frequently. On the last occasion that they did this, Coates claimed that Banner had asked him to put a belt around her neck and that she would pull on it and would tell him when to remove it. She died before he was able to remove the belt. He was found guilty of her murder and sentenced to a minimum term of seven and half years.

R v. *Connors* (2011): David Connors strangled Michelle Stonall in 2010. He had entreated her to meet him in a country park and he claimed that some sexual activity had taken place. Connors tied a dog lead around Stonall's neck and pulled it as part of the sexual activity. The evidence is ambiguous as to whether there was any sexual activity at all. Connors attempted to suggest that there was as an explanation for why he had used a dog lead to strangle Stonall. Once she had died, he left her partially concealed body in the park. He was found guilty of murder and sentenced to a minimum term of twenty-two years.

R v. *Doblys* (2013): Dainatos Doblys was dating Virginja Jurkiene when they took a hotel room together in 2013. In that room, they had what he described as very vigorous sex which, he said, she had instigated. The following morning Jurkiene was dead. She had died from suffocation and the effects of drinking alcohol. He said that everything that they did was consensual. He was charged with murder, manslaughter, anal rape, vaginal rape and attempted rape. He was found guilty of manslaughter and both counts of rape. He was sentenced to sixteen years in prison.

R v. *Foster* (2018): In 2017 Ashley Foster killed Megan Bills during a sexual encounter. He strangled her with his shirt and left her body to be discovered by staff working at his hostel weeks later. He claimed that the strangulation was consensual and the death an accident. He was found guilty of her murder and sentenced to a minimum term of twenty-six years in prison.

R v. *Gamma* (2018): This is an anonymised case. Gamma was charged, *inter alia*, with the rape of Enn in 2016. It is claimed that Enn was raped as part of a rough sex encounter, part of which Gamma filmed. At Crown court, he was found guilty of the rape of Enn. This conviction was quashed at appeal.

R v. *Gaskell* (2018): Jason Gaskell killed Laura Huteson during a sexual encounter in which he was using a knife against her neck to enhance their sexual thrill. He pleaded guilty to her manslaughter. He was sentenced to six years in prison.

R v. *Lambda* (2013): This is an anonymised case. Lambda was in a BDSM relationship with Aye. During an encounter he whipped her with a rope, leaving a large bruise on her buttocks. This, she said, violated her limits. He was charged with assault causing actual bodily harm and found not guilty by the jury.

R v. *Morton* (2017): In 2016, James Morton killed Hannah Pearson during a sexual encounter at his house. He strangled her to death. The strangulation was his idea, but she consented to it. He said she instigated the sexual contact between them. He said he did not mean to kill her. He was cleared of her murder and found guilty of her manslaughter. He was sentenced to twelve years in prison.

R v. *Mu* (2014): This is an anonymised case. Mu was in a casual sexual relationship with Dee. They exchanged a series of text messages which suggested enthusiasm for BDSM activities. She was found hanging from her bedroom window with him asleep in bed next to her. He said that what happened she did to herself and that he had no part in it. He was charged with gross negligence manslaughter and cleared on all counts.

R v. *Pi* (2014): This is an anonymised case. Pi and Bee were in a BDSM relationship with established safe words, limits and roles. On one occasion, Pi violated Bee's limit, causing her extensive bruising. She also claimed he penetrated her vagina and anus against her will. On two counts of rape and one of sexual assault by penetration, he was found not guilty.

R v. *Pybus* (2021): Sam Pybus killed Sophie Moss in 2021. He applied pressure on her neck with his hands until she died. This was a sexual practice that she encouraged. He pleaded guilty to the offence of manslaughter. He was sentence to four years and eight months in prison.

R v. *Tenniswood* (2016): Edward Tenniswood killed India Chipchase after meeting her on a night out. He applied pressure on her neck until she died. He said that it was her idea that he choke her. He was found guilty of her rape and murder and sentenced to twelve years for the rape and a minimum term of thirty years in prison for her murder.

3. Spectacular Consent

> Gamma: Tell me you'll do anything you [sic] want
> Enn: I'll do anything you want
> Gamma: Do you know what happens if you miss obey?
> Enn: (shakes head)
> Gamma: You're shaking your head (slaps her)
> Enn: No, don't, don't, don't
> Gamma: Close your eyes. Hands behind you. Now.
> Enn: (moves into position)
> Gamma: Arse in the air
> Enn: (moves into position)
> Gamma: Stay there for me … Say, 'Please'.
> Enn: Please
> Gamma: Louder, I can't hear you
> Enn: Please
> Gamma: Good (inserts penis)
> Enn: Ouch, ouch, ouch. Please, don't. No, please, no. Ouch (crying). Please, don't, please, don't
> Gamma: Do you want me to stop?
> Enn: (shakes head)
> Gamma: Say it clearly, say it clearly
> Enn: No
> Gamma: No, you don't want me to stop. You want me to keep fucking you. Say it clearly for me
> Enn: Mm-hmm (nods head)
> Gamma: There's a good girl. (*R* v. *Gamma*, 2018, p. 5)

In 2016, Gamma met Enn on the way home from a night out. She was with a friend; he was walking to get a taxi from the King's Cross area in London, UK. Gamma offered Enn a lift in a taxi back to a place in south London that he was looking after; 'she was interested in me, and I was interested in her' he said, in evidence … 'I feel like there was eye contact at that moment … She was kind of smiley and seemed interested to keep the conversation going' (*R* v. *Gamma*, 2018, pp. 39–40). The pair went back to the apartment and proceeded to engage in a sexual encounter which would go on to have sadomasochistic themes. Gamma was charged with rape and acquitted on appeal. Part of the evidence which helped to acquit Gamma was captured in the transcript of a film that he made on his phone (without her consent) of their encounter. At appeal, this exchange was presented as evidence of

Enn's consent and Gamma's reasonable belief in the same; 'she didn't give any indication she didn't like what was going on' (*R* v. *Gamma*, 2018, p. 43).

Consent – from the old French, meaning 'coming together to feel' – describes an affective sense of complicity and collaboration between consenting parties. Consent is felt, intersubjective – an active praxis of sorts – towards a mutually accommodating encounter. Or at least, this is what it might be. Questions of consent are at the heart of sexual encounters, whether sadomasochistic or not. Within BDSM practice, it is consent that is supposed to turn an assault – the slap that Gamma gave Enn – into an act that is permitted and that might be pleasurable or desirable. Consent is, as I have elsewhere suggested, cast as the *sine qua non* of BDSM (Fanghanel, 2020). Indeed, as I intimated in the previous chapter, it is what distinguishes BDSM from sexual violence and coercion (Weiss, 2011; Pitagora, 2013; Bauer, 2014). This is not to suggest that something that looks like BDSM cannot be coercive or abusive, masquerading as consensual kink (see Fanghanel, 2020; Bonomi et al., 2013, Walling-Wefelmeyer & O'Neill, 2021). Indeed, this is one of the points that I make in this book. For now, though, we can understand consent as something which is intrinsic to these debates.

WHAT DOES CONSENT LOOK LIKE?

In English and Welsh law, consent to sex is defined as something in which each party 'agrees by choice and has the freedom and capacity to make that choice' (SOA, 2003, s 74). In law, in the context of BDSM, questions of consent are less clearly defined. Assault is dealt with under s 47 of the Offences Against the Person Act 1861. These cases tend to turn around consideration of the seriousness of the injury and whether or not it takes place as part of an exempted category: sport, parental or religious chastisement, medical intervention, or tattooing/piercing (Bows & Herring, 2020, pp. 528–9). As we have already seen from Chapters 1 and 2, consent in any form is not sufficient in BDSM cases where harm has been more than transient or trifling. So, when we are talking about consent in this chapter we are not so much concerned with people's capacity to consent, their ability to choose, or how free they are to make that choice, but rather what work a concept of consent does in these cases.

Though critical of how consent is operationalised and imagined in many different cases, for Joseph Fischel (2019, pp. 3, 16), the way that it is imagined in law – a consent that is affirmative (yes means yes!), as opposed to forced, coerced, conceded, acquiesced to – is the 'least crappy' standard of consent that we can hope to hold. 'In law, then, let's not screw consent', he suggests (2019, p. 16). And yet, *contra* this, as the cases that are examined in this chapter show, sometimes consent in law screws with us, and maybe ought not to be afforded the *passe-partout* that Fischel's words imply. Consent is thorny, slippery, contingent. And yes, sometimes, it is also very simple. But it is thanks to what Heidi M. Hurd (1996) calls the 'moral magic' of consent that thinking about the legality of sexual practice becomes 'fuzzy' (Fischel, 2019, p. 28), or, as I suggest, spectacularised.

The moral magic of consent works in two ways; it transforms assaultive behaviours into something permitted; making something right, when it was otherwise wrong (Hurd, 1996, p. 123), and it provides an alibi for behaviours or practices which are questionable. If we believe in consent, we can believe that what happened was OK. In this way, consent can be said to operate as an illocutionary act. An illocutionary act forms part of speech act theory which shows how words do things (Austin, 1962). A prayer or the utterance of marriage vows are examples of illocutionary acts because they bring about transformation by being said (Bird, 2002). Consent becomes an object that is created by illocutionary acts. The illocutionary is usually spoken but gestures and non-verbal utterances can have illocutionary force, and bring something about by being performed (a wink to signal complicity, a nod to signal agreement). Consent as an illocutionary act holds a lot of power and enacts the moral magic that Hurd (1996) describes. Of course, the illocutionary needs to be received by the person to whom it is enacted – a yes or a no or a maybe must be heard as a yes/no/maybe – and the apparent failure of this uptake is where the troubles of consent can emerge. When consent is spectacularised the ties between the illocution and the uptake come undone. Sometimes cynically, and strategically so. We will see more of this in the next section. What these legalistic, almost contractual, understandings of consent do not do, is tell us anything about wanting, or desiring what is happening. To understand this – the *feeling* that is implied in the etymology of the word – we need to look more closely at how consent is iterated.

Within the sexual subculture of BDSM, the negotiation of consent is intrinsic. Consent negotiations are commonplace elements of the practice in which boundaries are discussed, limits established, desires expressed, and safeguarding measures, through the use of safe words and checking in with your partner(s), practiced (Jozifkova, 2013; Pitagora, 2013; Dunkley & Brotto, 2020; Bauer, 2021). For some, this sort of explicit dealing with consent is posited as a form of best practice for engaging with sexual encounters

(Galilee-Belfer, 2020; Angel, 2021). Of course, BDSM encounters do go wrong, consent violations do occur and BDSM practice is just as mired in intersectional power dynamics which can foster abuse as the broader world in which it operates (Fanghanel, 2019; Dunkley & Brotto, 2020). These failures of consent negotiations will come to bear on some of the cases discussed here. But, alongside this, not all of these cases which invoke consent are ones which emerge from an obvious BDSM-type arrangement or relationship. Many invoke BDSM themes and are BDSM-adjacent or are abuse which is masquerading as BDSM. What this means is that in many of these cases, there will not be a tidy pre-packaged discussion of boundaries, desires, soft or hard limits to point to. As Rachael O'Byrne et al. (2008) and Susan E. Hickman and Charlene L. Muehlenhard (1999) tell us, much of how consent is actually negotiated occurs is much less explicitly articulated (how much pressure should I apply here? do you like it when your hair is pulled? Can I bite your nipples?) and so, when trying to fathom the role that consent plays in cases of rough sex/sex games gone wrong/BDSM what we have to go on is usually hard to garner.

(It is also worth noting, that even within the explicit negotiations accompanying BDSM practice, there is always an element of consent that is implied. D. J. Williams et al. (2014, p. 2) note, in their suggestion that BDSM practice could be guided by principles that they call the four Cs – caring, communication, consent, and caution – that consent can operate on three levels. The first, surface consent, is more recognisably 'yes means yes' consent; yes, I like it when you pull my hair. The second, scene consent, describes what we are going to do together; first I will flog you, then you will go down on me, my safe word is my name. The third level, deep consent, is more blurry. What do you really want to do? I am crying but I have not used my safe word, do I really want to carry on? You said not to bruise you but now you are asking me to go harder, do you really mean it? The different levels of consent recognise that even with this potentially highly stylised consent negotiation of deliberate and thoughtful BDSM, consent is complicated, sometimes messy and, indeed, imperfect.)

The interaction between Gamma and Enn which opens this chapter reveals something of this mess of consent negotiation. Occurring during an already established sexual encounter, Gamma is videoing Enn in the bathroom. She is kneeling in front of him when he starts the recording. Enn's argument was that what happened between them was rape. Gamma was found guilty of Enn's rape at Crown court, but the conviction was quashed on appeal, in part because of the interaction that is figured here (other elements refer to Enn's mental health problems and her previous accounts of false rape allegations). Rather than the violent encounter that Enn described, this video shows something different. It shows some ambivalence. It shows rough behaviour and some play with power dynamics: her on her knees; him, standing, in charge – 'do you know what happens if you miss obey?'. She does what he tells her – the 'good girl' – she says 'please' when she is told to. On two occasions she says 'no' – in response to the slap, and to the penetration. The second time, she is crying. When asked if she wants him to stop, she shakes her head, he makes her say 'no' to stopping. She nods her head when he asks her if she wants him to keep fucking her. She is a good girl.

In this three-minute exchange Enn – in the submissive role – vacillates between appearing to want and to not want what is happening. Her affirmations are responses to his prompts, her refusals are spontaneously hers. He secures her 'yes' explicitly through the illocutionary act of a nod of the head, and yet this 'yes' only becomes so necessary because of the ambivalence of the deep consent. Does she really want this? Is she acquiescing because she is tired, or she is drunk, or she is in a house she does not know with a stranger, or because she does not know how to say a 'no' that he will hear? Certainly, he is entitled to rely on her 'yes' (and he does rely on it) but it is not unequivocal one. It is an example of the thorniness of consent.

One element that considerations of consent can overlook is the reality of this ambivalence (Angel, 2021) and the way in which consent, as a measure of what is OK, is an impoverished measure with which to identify sex that is wanted (Fischel, 2019). Part of what becomes at issue here is the way that some of these discourses rely on a heteronormative romantic seduction script in which men initiate a sexual encounter and women say yes or no (Beres, 2010). This miscommunication theory posits that men overestimate women's interest in sex, and that women display 'token resistance' – say no – before they say yes (Tannen, 1991). Rape and sexual assault are then the product of this miscommunication or failure of uptake of the illocutionary act of refusal (Cowart, 2004; Kitzinger & Frith, 1999). This miscommunication theory has been widely criticised as essentialist, heteronormative, and as rape myth endorsing apologia. And yet, as Katherine Angel (2021, pp. 104–5) deftly outlines, this dynamic of the 'no' which becomes 'yes' is not simply intrinsic to romantic scripts, from Mills and Boon to *Fifty Shades of Grey*, it is also a matter of preserving the self. Yes, women are invited to – incited to – want sex and to want sex which is rewarding, but 'a sexually desirous woman may become both the fulfilled wish and the hated object, and a man can simultaneously be avid and judgemental; aroused and punitive' (2021, pp. 104–5). In this context, where the man chases and the woman is chased, the chase itself becomes an expression of proper masculinity and femininity. Foiling this dynamic becomes an affront to both, for which women pay a higher price, socially, sexually and in terms of their safety, compared to men. Playing the game and saying 'no' before saying 'yes' 'safeguards men's feelings of power', which for some women is a safer place to be.

The fact of this dynamic, however much we may want to resist it and fight for a world in which all people could have sex without shame, is an expression of contemporary rape culture which denigrates women and normalises gendered sexual violence. It is further complicated when this analysis enters into a dialogue with Celia Kitzinger and Hannah Frith's (1999, pp. 300–1) discussion which demonstrates that refusals to invitations are carefully, complexly created but they are created in such a way that everyone in the conversation understands them. Their conversation analysis of refusals to invitations demonstrate that people refuse by using delays (pauses or hesitations), hedges (prefaces like 'uh' or 'well'), palliative comments (that sounds so nice! normally I would love to!) and explanations (I have a big day tomorrow) to say no. 'Yes' answers, on the other hand, are articulated in a more simple and straightforward way, including non-verbally.

In conversation, as Kitzinger and Frith demonstrate, people do not often need to say 'no' when they mean no, and they can be understood as saying no. Usually, silence, or palliative comments can achieve a 'no' that is heard (1999, p. 307). Even a 'yes' which means 'no' can be heard as a 'no'; 'in sexual situations we might expect weak or delayed acceptances to be heard as refusals' (1999, p. 309). Therefore, much as women might find refusing sex difficult, or dangerous, much as they might use refusals to enable gendered seduction scripts to play out (Muehlenhard & Hollabaugh, 1988), refusals themselves can be understood following the dynamics of ordinary conversational practices. We do not need 'no' to say no.

It is worth pointing out, at this stage, that the transcripts provided of court cases that I analyse here are in no way conversation analysis transcript. They do not capture pauses, hedges, hesitations, part-words and other elements that you will find in a transcript prepared for conversation analysis, known as the Jefferson transcription system (Kitzinger & Frith, 1999, p. 300). They are simple transcriptions of what is said in court. The mess of language is tidied up, and as I note in Chapter 1, they can be incomplete and sometimes incorrect words are used in the transcripts. As such, it is not possible to do conversation analysis with these documents. Yet, the points made by Kitzinger and Frith's analysis hold that refusals to sex can be made in a lot of ways, and usually not by saying a straightforward 'no'. Socio-cultural emphasis on the importance of 'no' facilitates an idealist turning of a blind eye to moments in an encounter where an unuttered 'no' emerges (O'Byrne et al., 2008).

Remember that even though we are looking at how consent is operationalised and put to work in these cases, in law, consent is not a defence to cases where someone has been more than marginally injured or, indeed, killed. And yet, as I noted in Chapter 1, claims about consent do some work in these cases; they reduce a charge of murder to a conviction of manslaughter, they affect sentencing minimum terms, and in some cases, they exonerate defendants entirely by negating the unlawfulness of their conduct (Edwards, 2015; 2017; Yardley, 2021). So, suspending for the moment the fact that consent is not possible in law, if consent claims do sometimes work to affect justice outcomes, what do they look like? How do defendants show consent?

In the case of Enn and Gamma, we are only able to interrogate the extent to which she said yes, or said no, because Gamma recorded the encounter without her permission. In all of the other cases that are analysed in this book, there is nothing as pleasingly explicit about women's consent or otherwise to BDSM/BDSM-adjacent practice. In many cases, this is because the women have been killed and therefore cannot give their account, in others it is because each side gives their version in court for the jury to decide. That is not to say that text messages, photographs, recollections of conversations are not used to point to consent, that they are not pored over to understand what happened, but nothing as crystallised as a filmed encounter is available to us. To search for consent in these cases, we have to look elsewhere.

From the cases that I have analysed, there are two main themes that help us to examine what consent looks like; consent which appears through explicit discourse (see Enn and Gamma above) and consent which just 'is' – consent that we are told exists but that we might only be able to perceive by looking for other indicators which might stand in consent. These consent 'black holes' appear over and again in different cases and are far more common than explicit consent. Both expressions of consent rely on rape myths to be legible as consent in court.

'THEY'VE INITIATED IT ALL, BELIEVE ME'

On a bitterly cold night in February of 2017, Charlotte Teeling took herself for a night out in Birmingham, UK, leaving her two small children in the care of her mother-in-law. She went out, we are told, 'with a real degree of uncertainty as to where she was going to end up at the end of the night' (*R* v. *Bailey*, 2018, p. 5). Though it was Friday night, the nightclub she visited was practically empty. She was on her own, and she danced, drank some shots of tequila and chatted to door staff. When the club closed at the end of the night, she went with the door staff to grab some breakfast. She had wanted to go back to one of their houses, but they refused. They already had people staying. She was, we are told, 'flirty', a 'bit tipsy', and 'not happy' that she could not go back with them to their home. She told them she was staying with family in Birmingham. They gave her advice about the first train to catch back later that morning. They parted ways with a hug.

Teeling then headed to a shop, followed by Richard Bailey, who had also been at a club that night. CCTV shows him approaching her in the store. They buy some drinks. They kiss. They hang around together taking some cocaine. And arm in arm, they get into a taxi to his apartment. They kiss some more. Her phone is used to watch pornography. By him, or by her: the user is ambiguous.

At some point after arriving at his place, Bailey uses Teeling's bank card to buy beers and cigarettes. She is texting her friends, her ex, and listening to music throughout this time. At one point, a girlfriend of hers calls her and begs her to leave and go to her house to sleep and have something to eat. She does not do that. Her phone becomes unresponsive.

According to Bailey, at this point, he and Teeling start having sex in a consensual and rough way. Bailey lived in sheltered housing and was visited by a social worker from time to time. On this morning, his social worker knocked at his door, causing him to panic. He had been having rough sex, went to check who was at his door, and when he turned back, Teeling was dead.

Bailey was charged with, and found guilty of, murder. He received a life sentence with a minimum term of twenty-nine years. His defence was that what happened between the two of them was an accident. Everything he did to her was at her behest. Bailey was fulsome in his police interview which is reproduced at length in court:

> Answer: We ended up having sex.
> Question: How did it start?
> Answer: I think, while I was on the bed already. I don't know how it started, but we ended up kissing and having sex.
> […]
> Question: And what happened after that?
> Answer: She started saying, 'Pull my hair,' and being rougher. She asked me to put – slap her and put my hands round her neck from behind, and this, that.
> […]

Question: She asked you to be rougher?
Answer: Yes.
Question: Were those her exact words?
Answer: Yeah, 'Do it harder. Fuck me harder,' this, that.
Question: So, that's what I'm saying, so was that her? Tell me what her exact words was?
Answer: They were that, they were that.
Question: Tell me again.
Answer: 'Fuck me harder. Pull my hair,' yeah, 'And choke me,' this. That I can, 'Choke me. Be rougher.'
Question: Choke me?
Answer: Yeah, but I didn't or I dunno. I dunno what happened.
Question: What did you actually do when she was telling you that?
Answer: Pulled her hair a bit.
Question: And how did you pull her hair?
Answer: Not very hard. I was too – it was too, probably, too scared.
Question: What part of her hair did you pull? The side? The back?
Answer: I think so.
Question: Yeah, and apart from pulling her hair, how did she react when you were pulling her hair?
Answer: I don't know. Seemed to be enjoying herself anyway.
Question: What makes you say that?
Answer: I don't know, I don't know. She initiated it. She was enjoying it.
Question: Mm, and when she said about being rougher, what did you do as a result of that, other than pulling her hair?
Answer: I tried to go as she said.
Question: In what way? What were you doing to be rougher?
Answer: Pulling her hair, squeezing her, tried to put my hands on her neck a bit, pull her head back from the hair.
Question: Where were you squeezing her?
Answer: The side – the side bit there. Hips maybe.
Question: What were you using to squeeze her hips?
Answer: My hand.
Question: How hard were you squeezing her hips?
Answer: Probably not as hard as she likes, anyway.
Question: What makes you say –
Answer: Cos she kept saying, 'Do it hard – harder.' Everything I was doing.
[…]
Question: Tell me about that. What did you actually do?
Answer: I squeezed her neck a bit. She was saying, 'Do that harder.' I was a bit nervous. (*R* v. *Bailey*, 2018, pp. 28–9)

The interview with the police runs to twenty-four pages. In this extract, we start to see how Bailey evidences Teeling's consent. She is the one who starts; initiated it, as he says. 'Pull my hair', she asked to be slapped, 'choke me, be rougher'. Bailey pulls her hair 'a bit' and pulls it 'not very hard'. He squeezed her neck 'a bit'. The minimisation technique used by perpetrators of intimate partner violence is recognisable here. She is demanding more. Everything he does is 'a bit' hard, the slap is 'light-ish' or captured within the vague 'this, that'. The consent is evidenced, here, because she is directing the action, but also because this is something that she seemingly really wants.

We learn that she 'seemed to be enjoying herself anyway' and later, when pressed on how he knew she liked it he replies 'by the noises she was making':

> Question: Was she – did she ever say no at all?
> Answer: No, no, no.
> Question: Did she ask you to stop at all?
> Answer: No, no, no, not at all.
> Question: Did she try and push you away at any point?
> Answer: No, no.
> Question: So, the whole time you believed she was enjoying herself?
> Answer: She was saying, 'Do it harder. Do this, that,' yeah. (*R* v. *Bailey*, 2018, p. 30)

Significantly perhaps, Bailey presents himself as only doing what he was told 'I would have done as she asked':

> Answer: Yeah, said all kinds of – well, she was saying loads of stuff, I remember that. 'Do it hard. Fuck me,' this, that, that kind of word.
> Question: Did that turn you on at the time?
> Answer: I suppose, yeah.
> Question: And did you ever use any words to her? Did you say anything to her?
> Answer: Not really, except probably, 'Okay, I will.'
> Question: You ask her to do anything for you?
> Answer: No, no. (*R* v. *Bailey*, 2018, p. 38)

He is subordinate in this encounter where Teeling calls the shots. This dynamic becomes an important part of how he tries to establish her consent.

> Question: You've mentioned that Charlotte seems to be the driving force of this. She's asking you to do these things. Have you ever done anything like that before with any other female?
> Answer: Vaguely, but I was a bit scared. I met this girl and I was a bit scared, bit worried to what she was asking to do, and I actually asked her, 'Why have you not got a boyfriend cos you're every man's dream.' She says, 'Cos they run a mile, basically.' So, no, not really well, yeah.
> Question: You've had experience before of another female asking you to do those things?
> Answer: Worse this one female was asking to do, but I was just too scared to do anything like that.
> Question: So, you've never choked a female in sexual intercourse before?
> Answer: No, I don't remember. I don't remember. Vaguely, I remember what happened with this chick in Leicester, but I was scared.

Question: Have you ever been rough in terms of when you've been having sex with a female?
Answer: Yeah, I have a bit. A bit, but they've initiated it all, believe me. (*R* v. *Bailey*, 2018, p. 43)

Teeling is the driving force, and Bailey has only 'vaguely' done this sort of thing before, or he doesn't remember, or, again, he has done it 'a bit'. The words with which this extract finishes capture his presentation of consent; this is something that he participates in, in response to initiation by 'all' other women.

It is helpful to bring this case into a dialogue with that of Marcus Coates who, in 2011, killed Jennie Banner in her flat whilst they were drinking and smoking drugs. Coates and Banner had known each other for some time and had some form of sexual relationship. On this occasion, according to Coates, she asked him to put a belt around her neck and she asphyxiated herself, causing her own death. In the summing up we learn from Banner's mother that she disliked having anything tied around her neck, even a necklace or a scarf. Evidence is presented from previous partners that she had no particular interest in paraphilia whatsoever. Coates's ex-partners were called to give evidence that he had, in the past, strangled them or constricted their breathing as part of 'consensual sexual foreplay' (*R* v. *Coates*, 2012, p. 7). He denied murder and was found guilty of manslaughter. He received an indeterminate sentence, with a minimum term of seven and half years.

Coates described the evolution of his relationship with Banner as follows:

> When we first met, we tried to become fuck buddies, but she didn't really do anything for me sexually. One occasion when we were both stoned through drugs, we did attempt to have sex, but when she tried to get on top of me to place her pussy on my cock, she only rode me for less than 15 seconds and we both realised it wasn't going to work. We have had oral sex, but she again couldn't get me hard. I have fingered her on every occasion this has happened. Jennie talked about having rough sex, we never did it, and apart from the day in question, never used ropes or any other form of restraint. (*R* v. *Coates*, 2012, p. 19)

In demonstrating her apparent consent, Coates himself makes the elision between consent and desire. He explains that:

> He went round to Jennie's, she asked him to put a belt round her neck. He called her a weirdo in a laughable way. He put the belt round her neck and sat down. She said she'd tell him when to take the belt off, and just smiled at him. He sat down and when he looked at her, she was going blue and he tried to get the belt off her neck. (*R* v. *Coates*, 2012, p. 15)

And when explaining the incident to the police:

> He had been with a working girl, she asked him to put a belt round her neck, he said no. She then put a belt around her own neck. He noticed that she started to turn a funny colour, he attempted to get the belt off her neck but couldn't do so. He said he didn't have sex with her as he couldn't get an erection. (*R* v. *Coates*, 2012, p. 17)

And to his uncle:

> He told him that she was a known prostitute. He mentioned not getting an erection on the day of the fatality. He categorically stated he did not put the belt around her neck and that she put the belt around her own neck. (*R* v. *Coates*, 2012, p. 17)

These events are recounted a number of times in the summing up, with only subtle differences. The evidence of her apparent desire to have a belt tied around her neck to 'arouse herself sexually' (*R* v. *Coates*, 2012, p. 6), appears in a few ways. First, as in the case with Teeling above, this was all her idea; she put the belt around her neck, or he did so at her behest. She could tell that he liked it because she was smiling. She had talked about rough sex before with him and called the belt her 'kinky belt' (*R* v. *Coates*, 2012, p. 20) and said that she 'liked it kinky' (*R* v. *Coates*, 2012, p. 19). In this encounter, we only have Coates's word for this. On the basis of other information about Banner's dislike for having anything around her neck, and disinterest in sex that was non-normative – she 'owns no sex toys or bondage equipment' (*R* v. *Coates*, 2012, p. 18), we are told – these events appear out of character, but, we are also told that:

> Jennie was someone who had, in the past, suffered from anxiety and depression, being an up and down person who could be impulsive. (*R* v. *Coates*, 2012, p. 13)

A mutual friend of the pair suggested in evidence that bringing about her own death in this way 'may have been her way out' (*R* v. *Coates*, 2012, p. 10), 'such was the pressure on the deceased that you cannot rule out the fact that she may have taken her own life and done so in the presence of her friend' (*R* v. *Coates*, 2012, p. 11), the judge reminds the jury.

A further element in both Bailey's evidence and that of Coates is that whatever happened to the women whom they killed, they were not in charge. Coates and Bailey are reluctant participants to their victims' lascivious demands. Coates distances himself from Banner's alleged desires. In his interview, Bailey mentions nine times that he is scared or found scary what he was being asked to do. He was nervous. He was worried. And yet he continued anyway.

Coates found Banner's request unusual. He called her a 'weirdo'. 'She then asked me to put the belt round her neck', he explains, 'I thought it was a joke and laughed, but I put it round her neck' (*R* v. *Coates*, 2012, pp. 15, 20). Coates positions himself as outside of the sexual – kinky – encounter. She is a weirdo, and so she is not like him. More than this, when giving his account he is explicit about Banner's sexual deviancy too, which also cast her from the protection of respectability. Though she had ceased sex work years before he killed her, references to her being a 'known prostitute' and a 'working girl' appear throughout Coates's comments and the judge's summing up. It should be noted that the interaction between Coates and Banner occurred, not as sex work, but as friends. Sex work continues to be denigrated, so the conjunction of Banner's history of sex work with these events serve to point to the possibility that Banner would have consented to kinky sex because, in other contexts, she is already a sexual deviant. The effect here, again, is to point to sexual deviance which functions to construct Banner as the sort of woman who would consent to this rough, kinky, BDSM-adjacent sex.

Bailey describes Teeling as 'every man's dream' because of her masochistic desires (which make other men 'run a mile' she replies (*R* v. *Bailey*, 2018, p. 43)). Twice, he mentions that Teeling calls him a 'pussy': an affront to his masculinity and an attestation of how demanding her sexual desires really are. When asked how hard he was squeezing her, Bailey describes, 'probably not as hard as she likes' (*R* v. *Bailey*, 2018, p. 29) because she kept demanding it harder. This aggressive sexual expression of desire, can be, as Angel (2021) reminds us, dangerous for women. It can explain how they get into trouble. Teeling's sexual excess is mirrored by Banner's sexual insufficiency. Coates could not get 'an erection on the day', she could not 'make him hard' with her mouth, 'she didn't really do anything for [him] sexually'. Thus, whether figured as too sexually exciting, or not exciting enough, the way that the femininity of both Banner and Teeling is presented, is as one that is flawed, and these flaws help to point the possibility of their consent to non-normative, deviant sexual practices.

Flawed femininity that is either too much, or not enough; sex work experience; actually asking – demanding – the acts which would lead to their deaths resonate explicitly with established rape myth tropes about the price to pay for performances of femininity that are promiscuous, or unattractive, or that challenge heteronormative masculinity, and femininity. They are sexual practices that are on the outer limits (Rubin, 2002 [1984]). Through techniques which minimise men's role in, and desire for, what happened, and by demonising the women that they did it to, the consent discourses here cast women not simply as consenting, but as actively wanting these encounters, without ever hearing their voices.

We see similar techniques employed in a number of different cases, too. In August 2016, Edward Tenniswood was found guilty of the murder of India Chipchase, but not before he explained that whilst he was cupping her face and kissing her in bed, 'she put her hands on top of his, moved them down until they were around her neck, then put pressure on his hands, and he responded by squeezing'. He was, he said, 'inexpert' at squeezing women's necks in sex; an act that he described as 'mildly kinky' (*R* v. *Tenniswood*, 2016, p. 19). In September 2021, Sam Pybus pleaded guilty to the manslaughter of Sophie Moss, whom he killed by applying pressure to her neck, 'an act that she encouraged and enjoyed' (*R* v. *Pybus*, 2021, p. 3). As is clear from the sentencing remarks in the Broadhurst case, we are told that Connolly, whom he killed, 'derived sexual satisfaction from being beaten quite hard' (*R* v. *Broadhurst*, 2018, p. 2), and that on the night in question, he had beaten her so hard that he wanted to stop but 'she made [him] carry on a bit more' (*R* v. *Broadhurst*, 2018, p. 3).

In each of these cases, the narrative that women have demanded rough sex, that it was all their idea, is accompanied by the notion that the men would not have done it had they not asked for it. The construct here of the submissive-but-active woman is mirrored by the figure of the dominant-but-passive man. The sub/dom active/passive dyad in each of these cases casts men as reluctantly responding to the sexual demands of women whom they encounter even as they echo heteronormative and patriarchal power dynamics between men and women. Mobilising men as the passive dominant further inscribes women as libidinally out of control with their sexual desire; men, the hapless pawns of these demands. This formulation relies on and rehearses contemporary rape myths. It becomes a cynical recasting of gendered power dynamics where, in the heterosexual encounter, suddenly women hold all the cards. This is a recasting which asks us to overlook that in the end, only the men are here to tell their tale.

Lambda and Aye were 'two mature adults in their forties' in an 'adventurous' relationship with BDSM themes (*R* v. *Lambda*, 2013, p. 2). In August of 2012, Aye visited a tattooist to be tattooed with the words 'property of Lambda' around her genital area. 'The defendant's idea, she told [the court]; her idea, he told [them]' (*R* v. *Lambda*, 2013, p. 7). After getting the tattoo, she was in considerable pain and when he texted her to say she would be 'getting a few lashes until she got the hang of being a good slave', she replied 'no, Please. No pain. Can't handle it, especially not now', referencing the tattoo (*R* v. *Lambda*, 2013, p. 7). He replied saying 'cool, there will be some pain, sorry, and from now on you must call me Mr Sir', to which she replied 'Yes, sir' (*R* v. *Lambda*, 2013, p. 7). He went on to whip her on the buttocks using a rope, which left a loop-shaped bruise on her buttock. She described it as 'whipping the shit out of [her]'. In police evidence, she explained that she 'knew what was coming' when she went to his house. This, the judge explains, is evidence for the defence, which suggests that the whipping occurred with her consent (*R* v. *Lambda*, 2013, p. 8). Does 'knowing what was coming' mean that she consented to what was coming? Is a loop-shaped bruise more than a transient or trifling injury? Is it something that can be consented to? Even though she said she could not handle the pain of whipping at that moment, is her 'yes, Sir', an actual 'yes'?

Pi and Bee agreed that 'she was looking for a master and he was looking for a submissive' (*R* v. *Pi*, 2014, p. 7). They discussed their safe words and negotiated her hard and soft limits. They chatted online about what they liked and what they would do for several weeks before meeting. After their first meeting, Bee said to a friend that it 'had gone well' and she had some bruising on her breasts and back, but that was OK. On the second meeting, Pi had, Bee thought, been taking drugs. The BDSM play was rougher than she wanted, involving strangulation. She safe-worded twice – the second time he did not stop.

> He tried to have vaginal and anal sex and forced it upon her, but he could only manage that for a while as she wasn't really wanting it and wasn't making an effort to enjoy it … He then grabbed a rod and rammed it up her vagina. She'd not consented to that. The more she closed her legs and said, 'No,' the more angry he became. She stared at the ceiling. He became more frustrated as he couldn't stay hard. In the end, he got what he wanted, but she didn't know if he came. At some stage, she had tried to leave, but he got her back on to the bed. She felt she didn't have a choice but to do what he wanted. (*R* v. *Pi*, 2014, pp. 11–12)

Bee describes herself as passive in the encounter, helpless, non-responsive. He forcibly had anal sex with her, causing her to lose control of her bowels, 'which made him really angry and he made her lick the faeces off him by grabbing her hair and getting her head down … She was retching. She'd never wanted to do that' (*R* v. *Pi*, 2014, p. 12). Pi, on the other hand suggested a different dynamic:

> He then got a bike pump and put a condom on it. He told her where to lie on the bed and he said he was going to put the bike pump inside her pussy, 'Slave.' She said, 'Yes, master.' He put the pump inside her vagina. He did not ram it in. He moved it in and out and she enjoyed that for a couple of minutes. He said he

> asked if she could take it in her arse. She said, 'No, master,' and therefore he then discarded the pump. (*R* v. *Pi*, 2014, p. 13)

Pi describes how they go onto have consensual anal and oral sex. When she loses control of her bowels, he then said to her, '"Clean it, sub," and she said, "Yes, master." She gave him oral sex and he said, "Good sub." … He said, "Clean it up with your mouth," and she complied' (*R* v. *Pi*, 2014, p. 13). The accounts that he gives of the same events as Bee place him as domineering, yes, but also respectful within the vernacular of BDSM play. She is a 'good sub', she enjoys the penetration – he moves the bicycle pump in and out to pleasure her – and when she refuses anal penetration with it, he obliges without fuss. The BDSM-themed interaction of the discussion about the faeces also positions Bee as willing and not acquiescing or being forced. We are told that 'she complies'; 'yes, master'.

Later, he says, they go on to have mutually enjoyable, consensual sex, where they are both rough with each other. She wants more – for him to ejaculate on her (*R* v. *Pi*, 2014, p. 14) – but he did not want to, he could not get an erection. Despite their different roles within the BDSM dyad, Pi's demonstration of consent paints both he and Bee as equal players in the encounter. She has already said she wants to be submissive to his dominant role. He gives orders, she is praised for following them out well. Her non-consent is expressed through full passivity, on the other hand. And one that he does not allow himself to be able to read. She enjoys everything that happened right up until he lost interest, and she went home. He said, 'he gave her her clothes, walked her to the front door, and kissed her'; according to Bee, 'she got up, dressed … and she legged it' (*R* v. *Pi*, 2014, p. 14).

Lambda, we are told, made 'ungallant, even cruel' comments about Aye's tattoo – a tattoo that she obtained for his pleasure. Pi explained that during their encounter, Bee saw on his phone a message from another woman calling him 'Daddy', which is an expression of erotic role play, suggesting that Pi had another partner. Though the defence does not need to provide an account for why Aye or Bee would be lying about the fact of their consent, these discourses of the jealous woman, or the woman scorned, rehearse rape myths of manipulative women who 'cry rape' when they do not get what they want. What is unusual about these cases is that they offer some insight into how consent was articulated and understood (not simply how it was negotiated) by the actors, which points further to how consent was then construed by the jury who then find these men not guilty.

INSIDE THE CONSENT 'BLACK HOLES'

The 'she asked for it' trope is a concentrated expression of the black holes of consent. So, whereas in the case of Coates, or Bailey, or Tenniswood, or Broadhurst we see apparently explicit evidence of asking for BDSM-adjacent sex, these flashes of consent visibility are accompanied by void-like absences of evidence of consent. In the cases of Lambda and Pi above, the women's withdrawal of consent could not be heard by the men, or the courts, and falls into a similar void. Most of the cases analysed in this book rely on what I have called a black hole of consent to be understood in court. When I started my analysis of these cases, I was struck by how often the defence would simply state as a matter of fact that women consented to the encounter that took place, and that this statement was never more fully interrogated.

When Jason Gaskell pleaded guilty to the gross negligence manslaughter of Laura Huteson by slicing her neck with a knife that he kept in his room to eroticise sex, the court heard that Huteson's consent (to the knife being held to her neck) 'is apparent here, it's not reluctant sexual consensual activity and it was straight consensual activity' (*R* v. *Gaskell*, 2018, p. 13). In 2011, Brendan Connors was found guilty of the murder of Michelle Stonall. He tried to raise a defence that the dog lead that he strangled her with was an act that she wanted. As part of consensual sex, we are told, Connors 'used a technique, at her request, of erotic asphyxiation, and the thing had got out of hand' (*R* v. *Connors*, 2011, p. 42). As part of his defence against charges of murder, manslaughter, rape and attempted rape of Virginia Jurkiene, Dainatos Doblys explained that 'the deceased had initiated sexual activity that evening. He said they got undressed; Virginia got into the big middle bed and asked him to join her there' (*R* v. *Doblys*, 2013, p. 32). In the cases of Pybus in 2021 and of James Morton in 2017, both of whom are found guilty of manslaughter by strangling of Moss and Hannah Pearson respectively, expressions of consent are equally simplistic. For Pybus, the pressure to the neck took place 'in the course of consensual activity' (*R* v. *Pybus*, 2021, p. 1) that Moss 'encouraged' (*R* v. *Pybus*, 2021, p. 4). Pearson was sixteen when she was killed by twenty-three-year-old Morton, whom she had met only that day and with whom she had drunk alcohol. He explained he 'didn't fancy Hannah' but 'was interested in sexual strangulation and had tried it out with a previous partner' (*R* v. *Morton*, 2017, p. 9). When the pair went to bed, they engaged in sexual contact, and he straddled her and applied pressure to her neck:

> She went, he said 'hang on what's this?' He stopped and said, 'If you don't like it tell me to stop'. His evidence was that she was fine and did not object. He said, she said 'okay'. (*R* v. *Morton*, 2017, p. 9)

Across a range of cases, expressions of consent are unexamined, or rather, are presented uncritically. The difference that consent makes in many of these cases transforms rape into sex and murder into manslaughter, so consent is utterly salient and yet here, it is presented to us as immovable, uncontroversial, fact. Yet merely stating that there is consent does not mean that there is consent, especially in cases where the consenters are deceased.

In these cases, consent falls into a black hole which either we cannot see or which we can only see in hyper-real, almost cartoonish form (the half smile [*R* v. *Tenniswood*, 2016, p. 14]; the 'kinky belt' [*R* v. *Coates*, 2012, p. 20]). In each of these cases we can only discern consent through other elements that suggest that consent may have been expressed. What are these other elements? When the existence of consent is presented as fact; how do we know? What does consent consist of? What forms does it take? Black boxed, this black hole means that we cannot tell.

As we saw in the instances of cases where women 'initiate it all', above, evidence of consent is accompanied by pathologies including a history of drug use or sex work. Women were undesirable because they were hypersexualised, owning sex toys, always asking for more, or because they failed at femininity they could not get their partners 'hard', or were unattractive. And, in cases where consent is a black hole, these themes emerge even more vociferously. Here, we see them take shape through discourses about promiscuity, vulnerability and stigma about mental health.

HORNY, CRAZY AND ALONE

In the middle of January 2013, Doblys and Jurkiene met each other in Wisbech to go on a date. They had been dating a short while. Both Lithuanian nationals, they had met via a 'lonely hearts' page of a local Lithuanian newspaper. We are told that they were both 'mature' – she is forty-nine years old, he is forty-eight – and they took a hotel room together. That night, they had what was described as vigorous and athletic sex 'on the floor, on the bed, on the table, everywhere, everywhere, sex, sex, sex, sex' (*R* v. *Doblys*, 2013, p. 42). We are told that Jurkiene is a 'rather large, depressed lady and a woman who liked her drink' (*R* v. *Doblys*, 2013, p. 18). She initiates anal sex, he says that they have sex all over the room, the sex is so 'easy' that Doblys 'describes it as like entering a bucket, no tension, no difficulty, no problems with penetrating her'. She dies of suffocation having suffered a significant number of bruises, abrasions and bite marks. Is it possible that Jurkiene would have the stamina to engage with the vigorous sex that we are told was consensual, asked the judge? His defence reply was that Jurkiene was 'sexually active' and, when drunk could be 'careless and irresponsible' (*R* v. *Doblys*, 2013, p. 46).

Moss and Pybus had been having an affair when he strangled her during a sexual encounter. Pybus was married but had been in a sexual relationship with Moss for three years. He was always rough with her, but he never hurt her, he says. Her enthusiasm for rough sex and consensual strangulation is 'positively supported by independent evidence from her long-term partner' (*R* v. *Pybus*, 2021, p. 4). Similarly, former partners of Dee who died during a sexual encounter with her cousin, Mu, were called to give evidence of her interest in rough sex. He was acquitted of her murder. Dee also worked as a sex worker. DNA from two different men was found in her vulva and anus on the day that she died, we are told. Elsewhere, in the case of the killing of Megan Bills by Ashley Foster, we are told that she possibly consented to strangulation because:

> DNA evidence from her trousers showed that she must have had a number of sexual partners, including being prepared to engage with Mr Foster in consensual sex when she had known him for just a few hours. She may have been willing to try something different, even if suggested by Mr Foster. (*R* v. *Foster*, 2018, p. 9)

In each of the cases of Gaskell, Tenniswood and Foster, the women they killed are lonely, we are told, and estranged from their families. Laura Huteson was 'a little distant from her parents' when she met Jason Gaskell on the day that she died. It is because she was homeless that Megan Bills ended up in Ashley Foster's bedroom at the age of seventeen. He strangled her and then hid her body in his wardrobe for over two weeks. Evidence presented at Tenniswood's trial paints a picture of Chipchase who, like Charlotte Teeling, had been left alone on her night out. She could not trace her boyfriend, she had been asked to leave a nightclub, her friends were all inside, she was witnessed by many people falling over and crying for a long while before she met and was consoled by Tenniswood who would take her to his house and kill her.

Loneliness and alienation are usually accompanied by the use of drugs and alcohol. Banner and Coates used drugs together and had been dependent on them in the past. Huteson had, the court tells us, 'fallen into drug use' when she met Gaskell (*R* v. *Gaskell*, 2018, p. 1). We are told that Chipchase was so intoxicated the night that she met Tenniswood that she had been refused a taxi ride and had been ejected from a club for drunkenness. In her drunkenness she fell over and hurt her head. We have already been told that Jurkiene was a heavy drinker. The judge reinforces:

> The deceased had a long history of alcohol dependency resulting in chronic liver damage. It's a rather sad catalogue, you may feel, of a lonely woman who's turned to drink for comfort, it would seem, on often occasions. (*R* v. *Doblys*, 2013, p. 4)

When Hannah Pearson was killed by James Morton she was 'significantly intoxicated', making her 'unaware of danger or less inhibited' (*R* v. *Morton*, 2017, p. 29). The same influences of drugs and alcohol were present in Natalie Connolly's body after she died. After examining her, the pathologist noted that 'he had never seen such high levels of alcohol and cocaine together' (*R* v. *Broadhurst*, 2018, p. 3).

Finally, promiscuity, morally questionable sex, loneliness and drug and alcohol use dovetail with observable mental health concerns, including suicidal thoughts in many of the cases. Mental health issues are offered up as further evidence of the possibility that women consented to the rough sex/BDSM-adjacent sex that took place.

Gamma was, on appeal, cleared of the rape of Enn, in part because of the video of their encounter that we saw at the beginning of this chapter, but we are also told that she had had significant mental health problems. She had been admitted to a centre for those in suicidal crisis, she 'went out of her way to hurt herself and put herself in dangerous situations' and was 'always putting herself in danger, found it hard to say no, there were lots of other times she didn't, when she wanted to say no' (*R* v. *Gamma*, 2018, p. 3), according to psychiatric reports. Dee was also suicidal, and the defence suggest, in Mu's case, that 'he was asleep when Dee took it upon herself to indulge in hanging herself for whatever reason, sexual or suicide' (*R* v. *Mu*, 2014, p. 12). Her past involved 'drug taking and mental health problems. It also involved suicide attempts and thoughts of hanging' (*R* v. *Mu*, 2014, p. 17) and though the court also hear evidence from an expert about 'how it is uncommon for people to commit suicide in the presence of another … and the pathologist, had never seen a case of suicide with the particular rope arrangement we have in this case around the neck', Mu was found not guilty of causing her death (*R* v. *Mu*, 2014, p. 72). Banner too, as we have already been told, was depressed, and the defence suggest that her strangulation of herself with the belt (as opposed to by Coates) could have been her 'way out' (*R* v. *Coates*, 2012, p. 18). Moss, who was killed by Pybus has also made previous attempts on her life (*R* v. *Pybus*, 2021, p. 2). The women killed by Tenniswood and Gaskell both, the court hears, have a history of self-harm. Chipchase 'began to cut herself with a pair of scissors, and bang her head and arm off the wall' at work once, when a customer in the pub she was working at made a comment about her weight (*R* v. *Tenniswood*, 2016, p. 7). Huteson 'had an unhappy history of harming herself and being harmed by partners. She was a victim of domestic abuse' (*R* v. *Gaskell*, 2018, p. 1).

In themselves, these observations do not become proxies for consent, and no court suggests that they are. However, the combination of these pieces of information – about sexual history, about drug use, about mental health crises, or about other vulnerabilities – in combination with uncritical statements about the presence of consent work together to build a picture of the circumstances under which someone might consent to be strangled with a hand, a dog lead, or a belt, or why they might accept to be slapped in the face, asked to beg for sex, or agree to using a knife during sex. They construct an image of the sort of person who would consent to these acts. They work to point to the black hole of consent which we can only perceive by attending to these other elements around it. Consent is taken for granted and unproblematised.

Gamma and Pi were facing rape charges, which raise different consent issues compared to assault and offences against the person. Though there were BDSM themes to the sex that the court ultimately agreed was consensual, the question of whether or not Enn agreed to be slapped, and Bee agreed to be bitten, is not considered in these cases. Consent to this, again, is taken for granted.

And even though it is not possible to consent in law to any injury which is more than transient or trifling, and certainly not to being killed, we can see that mobilising consent discourses does assist defendants some of the time. In the cases of Broadhurst (2018), Coates (2012), Gaskell (2018), Morton (2017), Doblys (2013) and Pybus (2021) this enables men to be convicted of manslaughter and not murder. Where the court agree that there was consent, they reduce the length of time that must be served in prison (three years and eight months for Broadhurst, six years for Gaskell, four years and eight months for Pybus). Dee's consent to rough sex, in part, works to exonerate Mu. Even in cases where claims of consent did not move a jury to acquit for murder (Bailey (2018), Connors (2011) and Foster (2018)), its very presence in the courtroom demonstrated that such claims have logic and are legible in these contexts. They still tell us something about how consent is figured and how we might understand this in the world more broadly.

Given that consent to serious injury is not possible in law, and given that notwithstanding this, consent claims still seem to function, or at least have some credence in the context of these cases, we should be curious as to what work consent is doing here. If, as Fischel (2019) also states, consent does not do the work that we think it does – and makes our thinking about sexual practice fuzzy – what work *does* consent do? What do these black holes of consent tell us about contemporary rape culture?

CONSENT AND ENCHANTMENT

As we have already seen, discourses about consent propel a moral magic which transforms illegal acts into legal ones. As an illocutionary act, consent makes possible this transformation. Consent education and consent literature will iterate again and again that all that matters is consent. Consent is intrinsic to ethical sexual relations. The fact of consent becomes a gold standard through which sex is legitimated. As noted above, BDSM practitioners – whether they practice in a community space, a club, online, or just at home – have an established practice of developing consent discourses and having consent discussions. Through negotiations, education, and attempts to safeguard sexual practice which has some intrinsic risk elements to it with safe words, people who practice BDSM might be said to have good consent hygiene. Some suggest that these explicit discussions can inform consent culture beyond BDSM (Galilee-Belfer, 2020; Dunkley & Brotto, 2020).

Indeed, there is much to applaud about the way that BDSM practice normalises consent discussions. In other jurisdictions, it is striking to see how representatives of sexual subcultures have been involved in developing legal understanding around these consent practices, enabling legal practitioners to better distinguish between kinky sex and sex which is abusive, coercive and illegal (DeLaney, 2023; American Law Institute, 2021). And yet, even these affirmative consent models become tricky to navigate in a practice which has some necessarily ambiguous elements to it (Williams et al., 2013). As we saw in the previous chapter, where in the USA, the possibility that a rough sex defence might be workable has opened up, in England and Wales, its impossibility has been confirmed. Belief in the moral magic of consent is ingrained socio-culturally, and as a microcosm of the context in which it exists, the courtroom is necessarily ingrained with belief in this magic, too.

Consent is enchanting. The binary logic of 'yes' and 'no' is comforting. Encouraged to think of consent as something that either is or is not there, we look to consent to help make good an array of situations. The power of consent as an illocutionary act lends consent to spectacularisation. Once it is enacted, its power to transform, in all the ways that we have seen in this chapter, becomes enchanting. Enchantment makes us less sceptical, less critical. We do not ask how things work, we just trust that they do, mystically or magically. Whence come the black holes.

Part of this enchantment discourages us from perceiving this complexity. It means that we do not look too closely at the construct of what enchants us. The ambiguities of consent, the grey areas, the resistance afforded by not knowing what you want are real – awkwardly so – but they are also hard to bear (Angel, 2021; Fanghanel, 2019). They are difficult to accommodate into discourses where consent is presented to us as 'yes', or 'no', and as intrinsic to sex that is 'good' (which is not the same as good sex).

Enchantment is facilitated by the way that consent is spectacularised, as is evidenced in each of the cases discussed in this chapter. The spectacle is the copy of the thing. It is not the thing, but it becomes the thing. The spectacularisation of the illocutionary act of consent rehearses, reifies and idealises ingredients of consent, and of its opposite.

In the cases that we see here, consent discourses rely on heteronormative sexual constructs of masculinity and femininity. They are also laced in neoliberal logics of blame, risk-taking and responsibilities. To consent to something is to make a choice about it. In other contexts, we see this too: the choice to continue a pregnancy, to working long hours, or undergoing medical treatment. In most choices there are elements to weigh up in giving consent – what are the implications of saying yes? What would be the implications of saying no? – and once a choice has been made in the affirmative, any physical, financial, reputational, psychic implication of the 'yes' must simply be borne as a consequence. Thus, the commodification of consent discourses – she chose it, so she must bear the price if it goes wrong – appears again and again. Through its manifestation as an illocutionary act, spectacularised consent becomes a commodity that can be used to punish, to excuse, to exempt, to permit the actions of the actors in each of these encounters. Creating consent as a commodity makes it wieldable as a defence, here. In the case of Pybus, Moss's previous practice of enjoying strangulation during sex responsibilises her for her death. In the cases of Morton (2017), Doblys (2013) and Broadhurst (2018), the excessive volumes of alcohol consumed by the women may have made them reckless, and more ready to take risks, we are told. It was her mental health problems which explain why Enn, in Gamma's case, accepted to run the risk of going to a stranger's house for rough sex.

These neoliberalised reaches are possible though the spectacularisation of what 'real' consent looks like. This consent imagines autonomy, freedom of choice, self-knowledge and the capacity to accurately measure risk as equally available to everybody everywhere. It imagines actors on an equal playing field, who are playing the same game, where everyone has agreed to the same rules. Spectacularised consent mobilises an idealised and ideological vision of what consent looks like in rough sex encounters. It is rationalised – preferably along heteronormative romantic scripts: he asks, she says yes – but consent as it *actually operates and emerges* is not subject of rationalisation. The fact of the complexity of consent means that is very much evades rationalisation (Jenkins, 2000), and it is the illusion of the rational which encourages us to believe so strongly in consent as an incontestable good to which everyone has access in the same ways (Pascoe, 2024).

Spectacular consent is weaponised in the courtroom. It is used to rehearse sexist tropes about sexually excessive women. It is used to erase the complexities of the conditions under which someone might consent to a sexual encounter – to get it over with, to make someone happy, to save face – and, in many of these cases, to obscure who can consent and who can be consented to in the first place. Weaponisation of consent makes possible something that is not possible in law. We will see more of this in Chapter 6. Consent, thus imagined, facilitates gender-based violence against women and sexual minorities. It discursively re-enshrines contemporary rape culture as the background against which these cases play out.

4. Spectacular Bondage

> 'Sticks and stones may break my bones, but chains and whips excite me.' (Spanner Trial protest chant, early 1990s)

The cases analysed in this book rely on tropes associated with BDSM to cohere with the logic of the courtroom. We saw in Chapter 2 that though rough sex and BDSM are not the same thing, they can look similar from the outside. As Martin S. Weinberg et al. (1984) have demonstrated, for BSDM to count as BDSM, it must be recognised as such by its practitioners. Alongside this sense of shared understanding, as a subculture, BDSM has specific attributes that distinguish it from rough sex – or BDSM-adjacent sex – which is less intrinsically tied to BDSM as a specific cultural phenomenon.

Certainly, not all of the cases that I have analysed feature a deliberate articulation that what is going on is BDSM, and those that do not rely on these BDSM tropes will be put to one side for now. Instead, the analysis in this chapter will scrutinise five cases which make explicit claims that the injury or death that took place between the male defendant and the female victim or complainant occurred as part of a consensual BDSM encounter.

When I talk of BDSM 'tropes' I am describing a motif or recurring theme that evokes an imaginary of BDSM that has coherence for people in the courtroom – namely the jury, but also other actors in the judicial encounter. Thanks to We Can't Consent To This (WCCTT) data, we have seen how the number of consent claims that are made in the courtroom have increased over the past few decades. On the one hand, this looks like an increased acceptance of non-normative sexual practices – a form of sex positivity perhaps; on the other hand, what sort of BDSM tropes are making their way into the courtroom? And is this BDSM as it would be recognised by BDSM practitioners themselves? What does courtroom BDSM look like?

GOING MAINSTREAM

> The defendant told you yesterday that some of their activities, their role playing, was inspired by a best-selling or sensational work of fiction which has spawned both sequels and imitations. You may be acquainted with it, you may not. (*R* v. *Lambda*, 2013, p. 2)

Lambda and his partner are not the only couple who will have been influenced by the phenomenon of the *Fifty Shades of Grey* trilogy, which spawned a film franchise and a number of novels and films in the same genre. It is well known that the *Fifty Shades* trilogy tells the story of a dominant, domineering man and his virginal, coy, trepidatious partner. A traditional romance cloaked in the guise of a BDSM love story, this 2011 publication marks a tipping point for BDSM as a subculture, and its presence in the mainstream. Sexual subcultures have always lived within, around and in dialogue with a heteronormative, and in this context, 'vanilla' world. They have a legacy of infusing each other. But the cultural moment marked by the furious attention that the *Fifty Shades of Grey* trilogy received marks the crossing of a Rubicon. In my own research about the interaction between BDSM and the mainstream, the near compulsory presence of *Fifty Shades* in people's account of why they were inspired to try BDSM is remarkable (Fanghanel, 2019, 122–3).

Representations of BDSM in *Fifty Shades* have been widely criticised as misleading, inaccurate, non-consensual and abusive (Barker, 2013; Downing, 2013; Bonomi et al., 2013). The trilogy is criticised for its misrepresentation of, amongst other things, consent negotiations (sometimes explicit, sometimes manipulated), the expression of sadistic desire (born out of childhood trauma), the expression of masochistic desire (absent, non-agentic) and mental health challenges (Drdová & Saxonberg, 2020). Each of these representations perpetuates caricaturised rendering of sadomasochistic activity. *Fifty Shades* has been rejected by BDSM practitioners as an idealist misreading of sadomasochistic desire as something that is 'unwanted' and 'forced'; a pathology that is weathered rather than, as most practitioners would suggest, voluntarily incorporated into one's sexual subjectivity (Drdová & Saxonberg, 2020, p. 11). The BDSM in *Fifty Shades* is superficial and operates as a vehicle to propel a much more conventional love story. Whilst the erotica within the novels might be outré in a mainstream context, it is nothing more than a heteronormative presentation of conventional romantic tropes (Tsaros, 2013, p. 875).

Notwithstanding the way that *Fifty Shades* has been rejected by practitioners of sadomasochism themselves, there is no denying the significant impact that the books and films have made on mainstream understanding of this sexual subculture. Though one of the most pronounced interventions of BDSM into the mainstream, *Fifty Shades* is by no means the first representation of BDSM to penetrate mainstream imaginaries. Bondage imagery has been used to sell cars, Nintendos, vodka, shampoo, mints, and appeared more recently and controversially in a Balenciaga campaign in which a child is pictured holding a soft toy that is trussed up in bondage gear (Weiss, 2009; Wilkinson, 2009; Beckman, 2001). It has been co-opted in awareness raising campaigns, including the People for the Ethical Treatment of Animals (Fanghanel, 2019). It is represented in films, music videos and performance art. The iconography of sadomasochism – whips, latex, leather, rope bondage – has gained traction within mainstream spaces. The ways in which it gains traction within these spaces, however, is through 'acceptance via normalisation and understanding through pathologisation' (Weiss, 2009, p. 105). The interaction is an uneasy one as it shifts the terrain upon which BDSM is understood as both sanitised and shameful, sordid and sexy, secretive and sought-after.

This interplay between a subculture and the rest – the mainstream – is significant in the forging both of that subculture, and of how it exists in the mainstream realm. The lines with which I opened this chapter featured in anti-Spanner[1] protest marches of the early 1990s in the UK. However, they are also perhaps better known from Rihanna's song 'S&M' from 2010. These collocutions draw attention to the deliberate and non-deliberate ways that the mainstream is penetrated by subcultures, in sometimes unusual ways.

Community is a significant part of how a sexual subculture such as BDSM recognises itself. Not all BDSM practitioners need to be active within a community context, but norms, values, ethics which are shared by people within a subculture help to define this group against the mainstream. Within the subculture, BDSM practitioners will define themselves against values and ethics of the mainstream, so-called 'vanilla' world. This might mean that a BDSM subculture could be more sex positive, open to difference, less heteronormative than mainstream expressions of sexual practice. In the context of BDSM, as we have seen, iconography around fashion, piercing, bondage have been borrowed in more mainstream contexts, but for a subculture to resist being subsumed within the mainstream, boundaries around what forms part of the subculture, and what does not – what Margot Weiss (2011) calls 'kumbaya kink' – are a key constituent of its identity (Drdová & Saxonberg, 2020; Gelder & Thornton, 1997). And just as elements of BDSM subculture penetrate the mainstream, the subculture is by no means a utopian space freed from what might be perceived to be the normalising tyrannies of the

[1] The Spanner protests took place in the early 1990s in response to Operation Spanner – a police operation that took place between 1987 and 1990 which sought to track down, arrest and charge men involved in consensual BDSM encounters. Operation Spanner led to the criminalisation of the men in *R* v. *Brown* that we encountered in Chapter 2.

vanilla world. Communities might value an emphasis on non-genital sexual encounters, communication, consent and care in a way that mainstream encounters do differently, but they can also be mired with misogyny, racism, body-shaming, whore-, homo- and transphobia of their own. They also have the capacity to be tightly hierarchical, with participants positioned within these structures attached to a cultural, social and erotic capital that is necessarily in flux and mired in mainstream norms about class, gender, race, age, ability and sexuality (see Fanghanel, 2019).

BDSM remains a stigmatised practice so, on the one hand, part of the work of the community is seen to be focused on nurturing the 'public face' of kink, with its emphasis on consent, education, and tolerance of difference. Broadening the appeal of BDSM subcultures might attend to some of the professional, legal, social discrimination that participants encounter. Normalising BDSM might encourage newcomers to the practice to understand how to do BDSM safely, and how to distinguish BDSM from intimate partner violence or abuse (Drdová & Saxonberg, 2020; Walling-Wefelmeyer & O'Neill, 2021; Jozifkova, 2013). On the other hand, part of the appeal of BDSM is that it is not mainstream; that it *is* deviant, different and risky. Not being seen, as a subculture, is exciting. The 'right not to make sense', following Jenny Sundén (2023, p. 12), to hold onto opacity as a political position, helps to ringfence BDSM subcultures from the highly visual – Instagramable – emphasis on BDSM aesthetic that is its prevalent face in the mainstream. The twin erasure and commodification of BDSM complexifies the specific experience of being a BDSM practitioner (Stiles & Clark, 2011). Yet, subcultures are also necessary to imagine other worlds, or ways of being (Hebdige, 1979). They nurture critique of the mainstream and 'of its dull and hypocritical patterns' (Paris & Ault, 2004, p. 403). Subcultures are, therefore, important social phenomena and require ongoing negotiation with the mainstream that they co-construct. Navigating this tension is a constituent part of any subculture. Commodifying BDSM through fetish-themed fashion, or club nights, or tourist experiences, or social media content displaces kink from its subcultural roots and fosters a more palatable, easy to consume, hyper-aesthetic vision of BDSM that, again, is only superficial. Spectacularised.

Alongside the aesthetic of BDSM, some elements of BDSM *practice* have also become more mainstream. In their study of undergraduate students, Herbernick et al. (2021) found that 79.4 per cent of the sample of 1795 had engaged in 'rough sex' at some point (acknowledging that rough sex is not necessarily BDSM). As Ashley Brown et al. (2020) note, the prevalence of BDSM practice is hard to state concretely. Whilst interest in BDSM is not statistically rare, and fantasies about BDSM are common, Brown et al.'s review of sixty studies of BDSM places participation at between 20–30 per cent of the population.

The influence of pornography might also be a factor in the prevalence of BDSM and BDSM-adjacent practice. Indeed, a recent British study has suggested that pornography which depicts strangulation and choking or 'non-fatal strangulation pornography' should be made illegal because of the influence that it has on sexual practices (Bertin, 2025, p. 19). Pornography has never been easier to access than it is today. The accessibility of pornography poses challenges to contemporary sexual practice, whether it comprises elements of BDSM or not. In their systematic review of studies about pornography, Dan J. Miller and Kerry Anna McBain (2022, p. 4) note that what is depicted in pornography can shape 'beliefs and patterns of consumers'. For that reason, it is important to understand how what is represented in pornography seeps into everyday understandings of sexual practice. They find that non-consensual violence in pornography appears in between 1 per cent and 15 per cent of scenes. However, studies into representations of violence differ in their findings; Anna Bridges et al. (2010) found that acts of aggression, including verbal aggression, were present in 88 per cent of the scenes surveyed from best-selling pornographic films. Like Fiona Vera-Grey et al. (2021), Miller and McBain (2022) identify that spanking, gagging and choking are frequently depicted in mainstream pornography. They argue that more extreme violence, including rape, is rare. Overwhelmingly, in what they define as mainstream pornography (accessible in mainstream platforms such as Pornhub), within heterosexual couplings, women are subject to violence and degradation, and they receive this either positively or neutrally. According to them, women are not usually depicted as not enjoying these acts (Miller & McBain, 2022, p. 10). Reviews of the content of pornography also helpfully inform what has become normative and what still is not within contemporary sexual imaginaries.

However, what these studies do not necessarily methodologically reflect is how people actually watch pornography. Usually settling on a niche, or specific representation of a sexual practice – humiliation, choking, or hentai for instance – users tend to delve deeper and deeper into scenes that depict these activities. If gagging, or rough sex is what a viewer is interested in, then it will not be a small proportion of the content they watch that will depict this, it will be nearly all that they see. Equally, representations of female sexual agency and desire are important, as these can be erased in legal and political discourse about sexual practice, though seeing women consistently respond positively or neutrally to violence or degradation, however spectacularly mediated by the screen, fuels the impression that this is what *all* women like.

Whilst Miller and McBain (2022) are at pains to point out that what we might do with knowledge about what pornography comprises is to enhance understanding about sex, sex education, sexual citizenship, there is no getting away from the fact that without an educative grounding in the context of pornography (what is it for? What is it trying to do? How is it trying to entice you?) and of sexual practice more broadly (what form does sex usually take? How do we tend to do it?), representations of pornography like these, alongside the ease of access of these representations, can have a deleterious effect on understanding of what consensual or good sex is.

Certainly, the increasing representation of sexual aggression against women in pornography might account for increased incidences of rough sex that goes wrong, and the increase in people who experiment with, or come to habitually practice sex with these themes. The partial and spectacularised way in which this happens also rehearses stereotypical tropes about what BDSM is, and how it appears in the courtroom.

JOURNEYS THROUGH PATHOLOGY

The history of BDSM is one of pathologisation. Richard von Krafft-Ebing was instrumental in setting about categorising human sexual practices in all their richnesses. *Psychopathia Sexualis* (2011 [1894]) is composed of vignettes detailing so-called sexual pathologies, including homosexuality, bisexuality and fetishism, amongst other practices. It was Krafft-Ebing who gave the name to sadism after de Sade (whom we encountered in the introduction) and masochism, after Sacher von Masoch. Suggesting that masochism is principally a congenital condition that is associated with degeneration as a hereditary trait (2011 [1894], p. 139), Krafft-Ebing notes that it is accompanied, in parallel, by sadism which is defined as the wish to inflict pain and use of violence (2011, [1894], p. 140). The two 'pathologies', as outlined by Krafft-Ebing, are detailed through the use of vignettes, reports from other therapists who were his contemporaries, and references to literature, poetry and other art forms where these desires are explicit. Sadism and masochism have thus been associated with pathology for the past few centuries.

In 1952, the American Psychiatric Association published the first Diagnostic and Statistical Manual of Mental Disorders (DSM-1), which acted as a standardising definitional source of mental disorders. Sadism was included as a sexual disorder, though it would not be until 1981 that masochism would also be included within the DSM-3. Inclusion within the DSM holds these practices as pathology-to-diagnose. Unlike nineteenth-century attempts to categorise sexual pathologies in order to determine the criminality of people presenting with those 'sexual perversions', the DSM is intended to assist in therapeutic interventions. And yet, as Patrick Singy notes, the cradle of inclusion within the DSM is often the courtroom (2012, p. 147). That is to say, a paraphilic disorder will be presented before the court where courts are asked to consider whether a defendant is 'bad' or just 'mad'. Thusly, disorders are sometimes diagnosed through questions of criminality. The evolution of the treatment of sadism and masochism within the DSM is witnessed in the DSM-IV and 5 which distinguishes between paraphilia and paraphilic disorder. Under this iteration, a paraphilia does not require intervention. A paraphilic disorder, on the other hand, does.

In the context of masochism, a paraphilia becomes a disorder if it has been present for more than six months and includes 'recurrent and intense sexual arousal from the act of being humiliated, beaten, bound, or otherwise made to suffer' and is accompanied by 'clinically significant distress or impairment in social, occupational, or other important areas of functioning' (APA, 1994, p. 529; 2013, p. 694). The DSM-5 also draws attention to the dangers of asphyxiophilia (the dangers of achieving sexual arousal related to restriction of breathing) (APA, 2013, p. 694).

Sadism is defined as 'recurrent, intense sexually arousing fantasies, sexual urges, or behaviours involving acts (real, not simulated) in which the psychological or physical suffering (including humiliation) of the victim is sexually exciting to the person' which have lasted six months or more, and where these fantasies cause 'clinically significant distress or impairment in social, occupational, or other important areas of functioning' (APA, 1994, p. 559). In DSM-5, the addition of non-consent on the part of the person with whom the sadist engages renders this a disorder requiring intervention. Certainly, as commentators note within the APA document, a sadist engaging in non-consensual sadism will continue 'until the person is apprehended' (APA, 1994, p. 559). The addition of non-consent as a pathologising element in cases of sadism makes explicit the ways in which sadism has come to be thought of as a consentable-to practise within psychiatry. Indeed, the DSM-5 makes clear:

> The majority of individuals who are active in community networks that practice sadistic and masochistic behaviors do not express any dissatisfaction with their sexual interests, and their behavior would not meet DSM-5 criteria for sexual sadism disorder. (APA, 2013, p. 697)

Likewise, in the context of masochism, someone who is not distressed by their masochism 'should not be diagnosed with sexual masochism disorder'. Thus, diagnostic tools leave the space for paraphilia to exist as interests, without the need for medicalisation of these desires. Yet, what the APA also note in these manuals is the ongoing link between criminal or harmful activity and the expressions of these desires.

Research into sadism has principally been undertaken with incarcerated populations who have been non-consensually sadistic, or from statistics about sexually motivated murders (which place the prevalence of sadism in defendants as between 30 and 75 per cent). Indeed, when criminal activity accompanies paraphilia, it is at this point that the paraphilia becomes a disorder, whether the perpetrator is distressed by their acts or desires or not: the crime is the disorder. When criminality becomes incorporated into diagnostic tools the different priorities of the law and of psychiatry become blurred (Moser, 2019). And as Charles Moser notes, the criteria for including some sex crimes into the DSM (e.g. paedophilia) and not others (e.g. rape) are unclear.

The reasoning behind some incarceration decisions is opaque – are people incarcerated for punishment? For the prevention of crime? For therapy? The eliding of these concerns makes for a diagnostic instrument that is at risk of misuse, over- and under-inclusion and whose political underpinnings are obscured. The relationship then, between the legal terrain and the medicalised one, via the DSM, is uneasy (Singy, 2012). And yet it is the DSM that tells us where problematic sadomasochism starts and where non-pathological sadomasochism finishes. To an extent, therefore, understanding this history of the construction sadomasochism as a problem (to borrow from Michel Foucault (1982)) through scrutiny of texts that have attempted to catalogue it, helps with our next tasks in this chapter; namely the slide from masochism, sadism to rough sex and sex games gone wrong and the ways that sadomasochistic acts are figured in courtroom spaces.

Accompanying this diagnostic history is a legacy of sexology research and psychoanalytic accounts which have posited that 'masochism is truly female' (Edwards, 2023, p. 3). That position legitimates rape myths which normalise the roles of passive/submissive female and active/dominant male within a heteronormative sexual encounter, and which normalise the idea that women want to be overpowered – raped – in encounters with men. Indeed, Susan S. M. Edwards notes that psychoanalytical accounts of women's desire, framed in this way, have been so compelling that they have influenced medical experts, legal practitioners and notable scholars in fields of forensics and pathology (2023, p. 3). Feminist scholarship has been steadfast in its work to demonstrate the misogyny of these framings of feminine desire and yet, as others and I have demonstrated, this psychoanalytically rooted account of heteronormative sexual encounters is compelling and continues to fertilise rape myths (Edwards, 2023; Fanghanel, 2019).

Holding onto belief in these dynamics influences discourse about BDSM, who is doing it, what they are doing, and why. We will see the implications of this influence in the cases that are analysed in this chapter. It is also worth noting that despite decades of work by sociologists, anthropologists and sexologists which detail the social constituents of what BDSM comprises, misapprehensions about BDSM, abound (Moser & Madeson, 1998; Weinberg et al., 1984; Weiss, 2011; Newmahr, 2011). Responding to Paolo Roma and colleagues' (2013) analysis of a double hanging that occurred during consensual sexual asphyxia through rope play, Ellen M. Lee et al. (2015) note that problematic assumptions about what BDSM looks like, and how it is done, continue to proliferate in academic discourse. In this case, two women had participated in a rope bondage game in which they were tied to each other by the neck over a pendulum; 'when one woman went down the other went up, thus causing a feeling of suffocation that was considered sexually arousing' (Roma et al., 2013, p. 896). During this encounter one of the women fainted, leaving the other suspended and asphyxiated. One woman died, and the other woman was critically injured. Roma et al. note that adequate safety precautions had not been put in place for such a 'game'; the participants had drunk a large amount of alcohol, and the male participant, who tied the women, did not have a knife available to release them quickly if he needed to. The surviving woman, they note, 'suffered sexual abuse as a child, had a history of illicit substance consumption … and sexual dysregulation' (2013, p. 895). Their conclusion is that BDSM is 'extremely dangerous'.

Lee et al. counter this construct of BDSM. They state that breath play such as this is considered to be 'controversial' within the BDSM community (2015, p. 1752). That is, it is recognised that there is no categorically safe way to do breath play. It is a practice whose risks cannot be completely negated. Where it is practiced, it is not usually undertaken without safety precautions, including the use of scissors to cut rope, and usually under conditions of sobriety. Importantly, they note, the pathologisation of the surviving woman as a 'sexually dysregulated' person with a traumatic history is atypical within communities who regularly practice BDSM (2015, p. 1752). They note, following Juliet Richters et al. (2008), that the prevalence of mental disorders within the BDSM community is 'no greater than that within the general population' (2015, p. 1752). The implications of reproducing stereotypes about BDSM as a subculture whose practitioners are pathological, damaged people contribute to the stigmatisation of BDSM practitioners who can be discriminated against professionally (Khan, 2014), in therapeutic settings (Dunkley & Brotto, 2020) and in law (Sheff, 2021).

Alongside the stigma of the BDSM practitioner as pathological, we also see scholarly discourses which erase the possibility of masochistic desire, and this also has implications for how BDSM is figured in the courtroom. Edwards's (2015; 2017; 2020; 2023) expansive work on rough sex, sexual killings, and how these are treated in court, highlights a similar problematic to that which is examined in this chapter; namely, how fatal and non-fatal sexual strangulation are a gendered crime (see also Yardley, 2021), and how similar cases are treated differently in court depending on how compelling defence evidence which 'traduces the character of the victim' is (2023). A rejection, perhaps, of the psychoanalytically informed tenets which hold that women *want* to be subjugated, that they *want* to be overpowered, a counter-narrative that masochism is a myth also emerges (Edwards, 2023, p. 5). Noting the increased normalisation of 'rough sex' in contemporary culture, Edwards describes it as a 'myth that women are masochistic and desire to be hurt and humiliated' (2023, p. 4). She describes as a 'nadir' an article in *Cosmopolitan* magazine which contains '85 best sex tips ever' because it reinforces the 'construction of women's sexuality to serve men'. Elsewhere, she suggests that there is 'no evidence that [erotic asphyxiation] heightens women's sexual libido' (2015, p. 28) and dismisses the claim that sadomasochistic desire is an enactment of fantasy; 'practices considered peccadillos throughout the nineteenth and twentieth centuries are now being positioned by some as lifestyle choices', she derides (2023, p. 5).

These views that desire which is masochistic cannot be true are echoed elsewhere. Citing a BBC Radio 5 Live-funded study, Hannah Bows and Jonathan Herring note that more men than women 'report arousal for … sadism' and that more women than men 'have experienced BDSM behaviours' to which they did not consent. In this study, 44 per cent of respondents who had experienced rough sex acts including slapping spitting, choking and gagging said that they 'always wanted' them to take place. Twenty-nine per cent said they were unwanted some of the time, 14 per cent answered that they were unwanted most of the time and 10 per cent that they were always unwanted; 'clearly the amount of unwanted "rough sex" is considerable', note the authors (2020, p. 533). Indeed. And yet, clearly the amount of wanted rough sex is also considerable.

It is important to acknowledge, as Bows and Herring (2020) and Edwards (2023) do so cogently, that more women than men are injured or killed in sexual encounters with violent themes (BDSM or BDSM-adjacent practices); that the perpetrators are almost always men; and that the dynamic within these encounters perpetuates the submissive female/dominant male trope. These dynamics are manifestations of contemporary rape culture. It is also important not to erase the reality of masochistic desire, even if this desire is problematic to a project of gendered justice. Simply stating that 'there is no evidence' that women get anything out of asphyxiation does not make their desire for choking or other rough sex acts less plausible or authentic. There is a more nuanced reality that must be reckoned with.

In a 2021 study comprising 4998 students of which 2453 were undergraduate women, Debby Herbernick et al. (2021, p. 1189) found that 42.6 per cent of women responded that they liked rough sex 'very much' compared to 38.8 per cent of men in the sample. Amongst heterosexual women, rough sex was initiated by them 35.5 per cent of the time, which means that 64.5 per cent of male partners initiated rough sex. Men initiating rough sex more than their female partners could look like rough sex is a male contrivance or occurs at the behest of men to which women acquiesce, and yet this dynamic – the male initiator – also maps onto time-worn romantic scripts about who does the chasing and who is chased in a heteronormative encounter.

The influence of heteronormativity is even more pronounced in Herbernick et al.'s (2022) qualitative study of women who had been choked during sex. In this study, women (who were all heterosexual) reported having diverse experiences of this practice. Some women reported accepting being choked to please their partners (2022, p. 1108). Some reported that choking 'enhanced arousal', that it was an expression of their desire to be dominated (or to dominate their partner); to explicitly play with the power dynamics of choking. Some enjoyed the surrender, the risky element to it and the 'pleasure, excitement, intimacy, caring and enhanced emotional connections with their partner' (2022, p. 1112). Though some participants did find choking sometimes 'unpleasurable, uncomfortable, scary' (2022, p. 1112), the erotic potential of vulnerability and openness to trust and belonging with their partner was also important. Notably, some women reported that engaging in sex which included choking was something which made their partners appear more masculine and more attractive (2022, p. 1107). Certainly, the heteronormative dynamics of these desires are problematically complicit with contemporary rape culture. Certainly, there are also questions to ask about how these desires emerge, circulate and interact with rape myths. Equally, some women are saying that they enjoy a submissive role in a rough sexual encounter.

Erasing the possibilities of this desire in the way that some commentators seem keen to, only allows us to tell part of the story of what is going on where women are killed or injured in a sexual encounter that is otherwise said to have been consensual. As we saw in Chapter 2, BDSM activists, scholars and practitioners already lobby for their sexual expression to be decriminalised in jurisdictions such as England and Wales (Cowan, 2010). Whether we agree with them or not, to deny the possibilities of a voice for masochists, or for those who desire that which is rough *to be done to them* is to engage with only a partial debate. This does a disservice to arguments which, quite rightly, point out how consent claims are weaponised to discredit female victims and to exonerate male defendants (or at least try to). Desire is not the same thing as consent. Folding the two concepts together, as so many of the cases here do, reponsibilises women for the events that take place, making a link between what happened to the women and the suggestion that *they wanted it to happen to them*. It also further stigmatises and alienates members of a sexual subculture who might then feel less able to seek out therapists, medical practitioners or legal institutions, should they need support related to their sexual practice (Lee et al., 2015; Khan, 2020; Walling-Wefelmeyer & O'Neill, 2021).

One of the reasons why this erasure is able to take place is perhaps because of the confusion of concepts such as BDSM, rough sex and sex games gone wrong. When Bows and Herring (2020, p. 533) report that women experience 'BDSM behaviours' they are, indeed, talking about practices which might comprise BDSM. But the key here is that the fact of non-consent on the part of women responding to the survey that they cite makes this *de facto not BDSM* (Bauer, 2014). The distinctions between BDSM, rough sex, sex games gone wrong, and what I call BDSM-adjacent practice is better elucidated in Chapter 2. For the purposes of this chapter, I focus on cases where an explicit BDSM practice is referenced and not a sex game gone wrong, or rough sex gone wrong, or BDSM-adjacent practice where the participants would not necessarily identify what they do as BDSM. Here, then, I follow Martin S. Weinberg et al. (1984, p. 381) in their definition of sadomasochism as something which must, amongst other constituents, be consensual, sexual, and undertaken as part of a shared understanding that what is happening is BDSM.

At the same time, what is clear is that even if parties involved in the cases analysed here are conscious that their practice is BDSM, the BDSM that they practice will be judged against a background where sliding between concepts happens. And here, it is the interaction of BDSM as a subculture and its penetration into the mainstream that is salient.

WHAT BDSM LOOKS LIKE

In 1984, Gayle Rubin's 'sex hierarchy' diagram positioned sadomasochism within the outer limits of the hierarchy. Alongside homosexuality, masturbation, pornography and cross generational sex (amongst other practices), BDSM is cast as bad, abnormal, unnatural and damned (Rubin, 2002 [1984]). Given the increased space that BDSM takes up in mainstream representations, discourses and imaginaries today, would it still be positioned there in this contemporary sexual climate? Probably. Though there is more awareness about BDSM and what it comprises (and what it does not comprise), as Eleanor Wilkinson (2009) notes, it is its 'otherness' that keeps BDSM interesting and obscure and deviant and 'out there'. When it does appear in mainstream representations it is often accompanied by a redemptive arc whereby though BDSM is an expression of a pathology, with the right person, with the right love, a heteronormative marriage union might still be possible to save the pervert from himself. We see this in the widely acclaimed 2002 film *Secretary*, and, indeed, in *Fifty Shades of Grey* (Wilkinson, 2009; Weiss, 2006). These partial, idealist, pathologising discourses about the politics of BDSM practice which have entered the mainstream are threads that run through the cases where explicit mentions of BDSM as a practice are the focus.

Five of the cases that I analyse in this work make explicit reference to what took place between the actors as BDSM, sadomasochism, or mention submission and domination. Alluding to these practices as occurring within the context of the sexual subculture of BDSM, they enable us to see how knowledge about BDSM, as opposed to rough sex or BDSM-adjacent practice, is constructed in the courtroom.

We encountered the case of Lambda above. Lambda and his partner make explicit reference to their interest in the *Fifty Shades of Grey* novels and engage in what was described as an 'adventurous relationship' involving sexual practices like whipping, restraining, body modification and control. In this encounter, Lambda was dominant – asking Aye, his partner, to call him 'Sir' – and Aye played the submissive role within the dynamic. We are told that Aye was 'enthusiastic' about her relationship with Lambda, that she was 'loved up', and given her willingness to tattoo Lambda's name on her genitalia, 'willing to undergo a degree of discomfort for the sake of the relationship … which she wanted to continue or resurrect' (*R* v. *Lambda*, 2013, p. 7). As part of their relationship, we are told that they had agreed to a contract as part of which she would agree to be tattooed in this way:

> It was one of her – what's the word I'm looking for – tasks, wasn't it, one of the goals that he'd set her, or they had between themselves set; the belly bar, the tongue stud, the written contract allowing him free use of her body until her birthday. (*R* v. *Lambda*, 2013, p. 7)

Penalties – the number of lashes that she would receive – for lateness, for wearing improper underwear and so on, were detailed in the contract. Creating a contract is not something that every participant of BDSM does, or is interested in, but they are quite commonly associated with BDSM practice. Indeed, in the novel which inspires Lambda and Aye, a master/slave contract is discussed. Discussion of the contract gives insight into why Aye was motivated to get the tattoo that she did, and also offers evidence that some sort of negotiation about what Lambda and Aye will do, took place. It suggests that what occurs between them might be consensual (the contract is clearly unenforceable in any meaningful way and is not related to the boundary that Lambda transgressed with Aye which caused her to contact the police about her injury). Expressions of submission though the surrender of control over her body – getting it tattooed and pierced, wearing certain items of clothing, giving him 'free use' of it – are also practices associated with a BDSM dynamic. That these were entered into enthusiastically points to the possibility of an authentic desire for this sexual encounter. It certainly seems to indicate that Aye consents to this dynamic.

After she returned from the tattooist, Lambda whipped Aye using a nylon cord, leaving a significant bruise across her buttocks. Describing the whipping, she said that he used his 'whole bloody force' on her (*R* v. *Lambda*, 2013, p. 8). Lambda agreed that he had tested her limits by 'deliberately [taking it] slightly over what he perceived to be her pain threshold'. He was charged with, and found not guilty of, assault occasioning actual bodily harm.

Likewise, the beginning of the relationship between Bee and Pi started well. We are told that they met on FetLife, a social media site 'for people interested in sexual fetishes … She was looking for a master and he was looking for a submissive in the Leicester area' (*R* v. *Pi*, 2014, p. 7). They communicated online and discussed their interests. Agreeing to meet, she brought sex toys to his home. They used the anal beads, and he whipped her, bit her and slapped her causing bruising. She reported to a friend that the encounter had gone well; 'all that happened was consensual and she was pleased that she had pleased her master' (*R* v. *Pi*, 2014, p. 9). On the second occasion, Bee visited Pi again, and this time the encounter went less well, leaving Bee feeling humiliated, 'unsafe and wanting to get out' (*R* v. *Pi*, 2014, p. 12). He penetrated her with a bicycle pump, he bit her, he raped her anally and vaginally, he called her fat, and when she lost control of her bowels on his bed, he made her lick the mess off. All of this, she said, was non-consensual. Looking at the bruising on her body after the encounter she said, 'he had massacred her body and used her like a piece of meat' (*R* v. *Pi*, 2014, p. 15). He was accused of two counts of rape and one of assault by penetration. He was found not guilty on all charges.

In both of these cases, language associated with BDSM helps to cast this dynamic as a specifically BDSM-orientated one with emphasis on playing with power. Lambda, we are told, 'texted originally that he would be giving her [Aye] a few lashes until she got the hang of "being a good slave" … from now on you must call me, "Mr Sir"' (*R* v. *Lambda*, 2013, p. 7). Similarly, in the case of Pi, it is explained that 'throughout this encounter she [Bee] called him master, and he called her sub' (*R* v. *Pi*, 2014, p. 9). Use of this language has the hallmark of BDSM-themes interaction as it is recognised beyond the BDSM community.

A common theme between these two cases is that dominant actors push the limits of the submissive participants. Pi and Bee, we are told, negotiated their limits:

> she had hard limits and did not want any marks which would show outside her nurse's uniform, nor did she want a threesome with a friend. Strangulation was a hard limit and was covered in her wish for no visible marks outside her uniform. (*R* v. *Pi*, 2014, p. 7)

On the occasion that caused Bee such distress, her breasts had been so badly bruised that her friend – who was also a nurse – was 'shocked' by them. Bee was 'distressed and traumatised' by what had happened and said that she had not consented to it. Similarly, Lambda pushed the limit of what Aye could bear, and, importantly acknowledged that he did this deliberately. As D. J. Williams et al. (2013) suggest, and as we saw in Chapter 2, when consent is negotiated, there remains the interplay between what people say they want, and how far they are willing to go; the difference between surface consent and scene consent. Sometimes, and with prior discussion, some boundary testing or pushing is part of the appeal of BDSM practice. On a different occasion, Pi had tried to push Bee's boundaries but had remained within the limits of what she would abide at that moment:

> He told her, 'Would sub like anal?' and she said, 'No, master,' and anal sex did not take place. He asked for oral sex, and she complied. She explained that a master should be caring towards his sub. (*R* v. *Pi*, 2014, p. 9)

Staci Newmahr (2011) has defined this pushing of boundaries as a form of edgework, meaning that testing the limits, going up to, pushing, but not transcending the edge is part of the play that some dominant and submissive partners will be seeking. The success of this edgework relies on expertise of the actors, especially the dominant ones, but also on communication, including – especially – non-verbal communications. In Lambda's case, Aye had been clear that she was not in the frame of mind for any painful sensations after her tattoo was finished.

> she replied almost immediately, less than two minutes later, 'No, please. No pain. Can't handle it, especially not now. Can't sit, can't bend, can't walk probably. It's bloody sore', a reference to the tattoo, presumably. (*R* v. *Lambda*, 2013, p. 7)

Yet, within a BDSM encounter where playing with power dynamics may be taking place, 'yes' and 'no' do not always mean the same things that they mean outside of that encounter. When it comes to playing with limits, attending to communication is important. And yet only attending to what is communicated has its own issues.

Pi's partner, Bee, had told him that

> She was fine with hair pulling, light biting, and spanking provided it didn't leave a mark. They had normal vaginal sex, but a bit rougher and anal sex occasionally using a lubricant which she consented to once in a while but not all the time … She said that this type of sex relies on trust. (*R* v. *Pi*, 2014, p. 7)

After the encounter for which Pi was on trial, Bee went to work, and after her shift, texted him to apologise for being a 'crap sub', and though they did not meet again, they did exchange some messages. The apology, and the continued communication could be framed as an indication of Bee's self-blame for the crossing of her boundaries. Later, in a conversation about the event with her friend, she said of her bruising that it was her 'own fault. Should have safe worded sooner'. Bee's evidence makes an appeal to principles of BDSM practice – hard limits, trust, being a 'good' or 'bad' sub – which suggest engagement with BDSM subcultural norms. Yet, her self-blame around the use of her safe word also demonstrates how narratives of victim-blaming, of who is responsible for what happens when things go wrong, also permeate her understanding of what took place.

Safe words are used to influence dynamics within BDSM play. They are usually words that are out of context for the scene, and which indicate that activity should stop, slow down, or change. Bee's safe words were 'red' for stop, and 'yellow' for slow down. She and Pi had used safe words successfully before:

> he started to strangle her which was one of her hard limits. In other words, she didn't like it. So, she used her safe word 'red' which meant he had to stop, and he did stop. She said she didn't like it, and he apologised. (*R* v. *Pi*, 2014, p. 11)

Later, however, he did not stop when she used her safe word and it was at that point that for her, the encounter became non-consensual. When safe words are discussed in a court setting, their function appears to be well understood:

> Defence: that idea of the safe word, which may not mean – mean much to a lot of people, but in their environment it – it provides a safety net of sorts.
>
> Judge: And what appears to be the position is that if a person who is indulging in this form of activity mentions whatever this word is, I mean, the other participant in the consensual activity is supposed to stop. (*R* v. *Gaskell*, 2018, p. 15)

In a different case which featured consensual BDSM themes, Jason Gaskell cut Laura Huteson's neck whilst they were having sex. Knife play is a higher risk BDSM practice in which a knife is used to simulate threat, to add pressure to the skin, or to scratch and tease the body. In 2018, Gaskell pleaded guilty to gross negligence manslaughter. Huteson, whom he killed, had only met him earlier that evening. At his home, which he shared with friends, they drank alcohol, he took some cocaine, and they spent what appeared to be an enjoyable time together, during which they had sex, including, on at least one occasion, using the knife that the court heard he kept in his room for 'this form of sexual activity' which the judge identifies as being a 'form of sado-masochistic sex' (*R* v. *Gaskell*, 2018, p. 3).

Gaskell and Huteson had established the use of a safe word. In evidence, one of his housemates explained that at some point during the brief time that they all knew each other, Huteson had become upset:

> [Witness:] I asked her [in other words Huteson] what was wrong, and she told me that during intercourse with Jason he had strangled her and she safe-worded on him because she couldn't breathe and he didn't stop. She didn't think he was going to stop but eventually he did. I just – I didn't think, like, I know

> Jason's a bit rough in the bedroom. I just thought it was that. I didn't think he'd meant to do it.
>
> Judge: But they – they – he did use what is called a 'safe word', so that the other participant in the consensual sadomasochistic activity could say 'stop' or whatever the word is – and he eventually did stop. (*R* v. *Gaskell*, 2018, p. 7)

The function of the safe word, here, is well understood. However, merely having a safe word alone is not enough to ensure that sexual encounters remain consensual, or safe. In this sentencing discussion, the judge is convinced by the safe word, mentioning four times that this safe word mechanism was in place: 'at least they had the safe word system, if you like' (*R* v. *Gaskell*, 2018, p. 14). How safe words are responded to in an encounter may vary from context to context. A key element is, however, that it is an expression that something has to stop, or change. Another key element of the discussion that appears to be overlooked in the account given by Gaskell's housemate here, is not that there was a safe word, but that the safe word was not respected. She 'safe-worded' and he did not stop. Rather than an indication that this is BDSM practice that is risk-aware, it could also be read as BDSM practice which is careless, and which does not attend to the risks inherent in BDSM practice using breath play – 'strangling' as Huteson put it – or, indeed, knife play, which was how she was ultimately killed.

What does BDSM look like when it appears in court? We see that language and artefacts associated with BDSM have, in some ways, penetrated those mainstream space. The accoutrements of kink, the slave contract, the rope, whips, sex toys, work to signal a deliberate interest on the behalf of the participants in something intentionally kinky. The use of names like sub, slave, Master, Dom; the concept of limits, what they are, and what they mean, also emerged here; safe words are also understood within this framework as mechanisms which are intended to safeguard participants from some risk of harm, injury or other negative outcome. The 'what' of BDSM in the courtroom is clearer. The 'who', and the 'why' also tell us about how BDSM is understood in the courtroom.

WHO DOES BDSM? AND WHY DO THEY DO IT?

> I scare myself the sort of dirty sex into, it would warp your mind. (*R* v. *Mu*, 2014, p. 23)

Dee was in a sexual relationship with her cousin Mu. He was in her bed when her partially dressed body was discovered hanging by a rope slung over the window frame of her bedroom. Mu was charged with manslaughter and assault occasioning actual bodily harm. He was found not guilty. Dee, we are told seventeen times in the judge's summing up, was interested in sadomasochism:

> There is much surrounding evidence to suggest she was interested in sexual – correction – sadomasochistic sexual activity ... there are a number of text messages in [the evidence pack] which reveal interest in violent sex. (*R* v. *Mu*, 2014, p. 21)

Her interest in BDSM was demonstrated in evidence given by men who had had sexual relationships with her. 'She got off on being choked', says one (*R* v. *Mu* 2014, p. 22), 'she suggested rough sex, which he said put him off' says another. A third who used to pay Dee for sex said, 'I had sex with Dee twice and during one of them, Dee asked me to put a belt around her neck. I was having sex with her from behind when she said this. I replied something like, "What you on about?" and carried on ... Dee, I thought at the time, was just sex mad' (*R* v. *Mu*, 2014, p. 22).

Dee and Mu also exchanged a considerable quantity of text messages detailing the sadomasochistic sex that they wanted to have:

> 'I'm gonna knob you daft, then make your face all sticky and jizzle on your titties, mouth and hair. Want to tie you up and sex slave you up as well'. Her reply, a short while later, 'You tie me up and rape me at knifepoint' (*R* v. *Mu*, 2014, p. 26)

> 'The harder you push your knob in my mouth the better, I pass out the better. I get screw, all good in the hood for me', and then she says, 'Are you not down for slashing me up while we do this good stuff?' And then he responds about 20 minutes before midnight, 'I'm all fucking hard and horny now but gonna save it all up for you, take all my frustration out on you. You're gonna get it hard and good soon', and then he says, 'If you want slash up, I will. You tell me how far to go. I beat shit out of you if I want'. (*R* v. *Mu*, 2014, p. 26)

Their conversations detail fantasies of what they would like to do together which feature themes of violence, 'torture' in her words, and bodily harms such as cutting, burning and beatings.

As we have seen, BDSM has a pathologised history and despite its entry into mainstream arenas, some representations of it continue to frame it as a pathology and expression of sexual deviance.

Early in the judge's comments we are told that:

> She had an interest, it would seem, in sadomasochist sex. He has told you he did not. (*R* v. *Mu*, 2014, p. 18)

Demonstrated by the text messages that they exchanged, Dee's interest in BDSM activity appears evident. The way in which this interest is treated in court gives us insight into how BDSM is 'known'. Indeed, as we see above, the judge's comments elide BDSM with 'violent sex' which is a spectacularisation and flattening of the specific role that what appears to be violence plays within the subculture. Moreover, this is an interest that only she has, explaining that for his part, Mu was drunk when he was responding to Dee and he had no interest in BDSM. Previous partners dismiss her as 'sex mad'. The deviance of her desire also becomes aligned with other non-normative sexual practices:

> she seemingly gave sexual favours for either money or drugs. It appears the defendant had no problem with knowing his cousin was indulging in this lifestyle. (*R* v. *Mu*, 2014, pp. 5–6)

Reference to Dee's sex work is made a number of times in the judge's comments. That Dee and Mu were cousins is also emphasised. Dee herself referred to their sexual relationship as their 'dirty secret' (*R* v. *Mu*, 2014, p. 24). Certainly, entering into a sexual relationship with a cousin harbours seedy connotations. These associations help to align BDSM interest with other pathologies associated with drugs, alcohol and, as we also come to understand, promiscuity. Later in the summing up, we are told that autopsy records attest that:

> Her mouth, anal and vaginal swabs were examined for semen to see whether and, if so, with whom Dee may have had sexual intercourse. No semen was found in the mouth, low vaginal and high vaginal swabs whilst a trace of semen was found in the anal and vulval swabs. DNA testing was undertaken, and it appeared that the DNA revealed that there was material from the deceased, obviously, the defendant and another person. It is impossible, of course, to say who that other person was. (*R* v. *Mu*, 2014, p. 45)

Dee died by hanging in her bedroom with Mu in bed next to her. The sexual contact that she had with the unnamed third person is only relevant to the circumstances of her death insofar as it helps to paint a picture of the conduct that Dee engaged in. Certainly, it confirms evidence that she had had sex for money earlier in the day but is not salient to her cause of death. By reminding the jury of the fact that Dee had potentially had sexual intercourse with more than one man in the same day, they help to make the elision between the idea of sadomasochistic desire and potentially indiscriminate sexual conduct; conduct which stands outside of mainstream sexual practice against a background of heteronormative sexual mores. The linking of these ideas also works to paint a picture of the sort of person who is interested in sadomasochism. This construct is rendered even more explicit because it is contrasted against the attitude of Mu who maintains that the sex they had was always, in his words, 'normal'; 'There was sex, oral sex and normal sex' (*R* v. *Mu*, 2014, p. 34). For Mu, the text messages that he sent were 'drunken, sexual chat which he never put into practice'. Dee's sordid and perverse desires are all her own. He, unlike Dee, was 'normal'.

Willingness to take risks, to push the limits of what is 'normal' is also offered as an account for what happened between Gamma and Enn, whom we met in Chapter 3. In that case, Enn gives an account of a violent encounter in which Gamma anally and vaginally rapes her and hits her as part of a BDSM encounter. The judge summarised the evidence Gamma has offered to the court:

> 'She took my hand and put it on her throat, and she pressed down and she said, "I like that."'
>
> 'I said to her, "I think you are submissive dominance, kind of thing. Do you like that?" Her response was that she said she did. She said, "I do." … I think she said, "Yeah." Up to that point, nothing happened that she didn't appear to like … She gave me no sign that she didn't want to follow my lead … I thought she was completely willing and turned on by it.'
>
> Question, 'Why did you think it was appropriate with someone you hadn't known?' Answer, 'I've been asking myself that as well and I think that's a mistake because I didn't know her, I really didn't know her at all.'
>
> Question, 'What, at the time, led you to think that you could even ask?' Answer, 'Only that she, we had just met and she [inaudible] come back to mine and after getting together downstairs to come up to bed, well, she clearly was adventurous on some level as not that usual.' I suppose it is not that usual to go straight back to the house. 'It didn't strike me as unusual that she was happy to do so, but looking back, I don't think I realised what risk that took as I didn't know her.' (*R* v. *Gamma*, 2018, pp. 41–2)

Gamma is clear that Enn instigates the power play, and that he then takes the lead in the action, adopting a dominant role. This interchange between Gamma and his defence barrister tells us more about who does BDSM, or a 'submissive dominant kind of thing'. Why did he think it was appropriate? Why did he think he could even ask Enn if she would be up for it? Because, 'unusually', she agreed to be taken back to his house with him. She agreed to get into bed with him. Her 'adventurousness' in one context was read by Gamma to imply that she would be happy to engage in BDSM with a stranger. Her 'adventurousness', or risk-taking, or recklessness, accounts for her agreement. It is worth noting how the defence casts non-normative sexual practice as something inappropriate to 'even ask for', which rehearses sex negative constructions of good sex and sex which is bad, kinky, and with a stranger. It is also worth noting how risk-taking narratives are figured, here. It is Enn, like Aye before her, who is cast as 'adventurous'.

Before it was associated with boldness and excitement, 'adventurousness' was a term used in the mid-fourteenth century to describe a hazardous thing or accidental event. Transformed into meaning 'daring, bold, and hardy', adventurousness and daring can be essentialised along hetero-masculinist lines and yet here, it is the women who are adventurous. Adventurers are brave, overcome obstacles and transcend challenges. Adventurers take on the mantle of adventure themselves; it is something that they have chosen; they are responsible for what happens. Enn's adventurousness, according to Gamma, victimises him. He sees that it was 'a mistake' to have sex with her, he, *not she*, took the risk by bringing her home. By accusing him of rape, he became in danger. A danger that he knows about, presumably, because of women who 'cry rape'. It is a perversion of victimisation discourses about rape. Her willingness to engage in adventurous sex with him, having only just met him, is perilous to *him*, and not the other way around.

Mental health issues are put into a dialogue with sadomasochistic tendencies to tell stories about who does BDSM and why. We are told that in her evidence Enn stated:

> 'There was no discussion about dominant sex that I remember.' It was put to her by [the defence] that a safe word was agreed. It was 'bells.' 'No,' said Enn. Then [the defence] explored Enn's mental health history. You have got the details of that, I do not need to go through that and then [the defence] asked, 'Why didn't you leave?' Answer, 'He told me that if I complained, he'd make it worse for me,' and she said, 'At the end, before he went to sleep and I was crying and upset', he said, 'You've got it wrong.' (*R* v. *Gamma*, 2018, p. 38)

Elsewhere, Enn's mental health history is explained at length. We hear from her psychologist that:

> She often goes off with strangers and takes whatever drug they have, lets people do what they want to her, switches off … She found it hard to say 'no' to people … She goes out and if someone chats to her, she will have sex with strangers. I asked her what she was thinking when she did this, and she said she hates herself and feels she deserves no better. In a way, when she's out walking late at night, if she gets murdered it won't look like suicide … She said she wasn't exactly planning suicide but putting herself in dangerous situations would save her having to do it. I got the sense she could quite easily throw herself under a tube or walk out into traffic … She said she went out of her way to hurt herself and put herself in dangerous situations. When she said 'no' she felt like she didn't have the right to say 'no' and even when she did, she wasn't listened to … (*R* v. *Gamma*, 2018, p. 10)

Enn's suicidal thoughts and deliberately reckless behaviour appear here to provide a context for why she has ended up with Gamma at the end of the night. Once more, her promiscuity, coupled with her mental health issues, rehearse stereotyped constructions of people who might be interested in sadomasochism. They are put to work by the defence to undermine the reliability of Enn's evidence. Gamma's conviction was overturned on appeal.

We also see this in the context of Dee's case:

> The background is, you may feel, extremely sad, perhaps tragic, for Dee. It involved drug taking and mental health problems. It also involved suicide attempts and thoughts of hanging. (*R* v. *Mu*, 2014, p. 18)

Later, we are told that:

> both [her children] witnessed Dee trying to suffocate herself with a plastic bag over her head. [evidence] goes on to recall other occasions when family members indicated that Dee was trying to kill herself and wanted to commit suicide. (*R* v. *Mu*, 2014, p. 18)

Dee's mental health issues and suicidal thoughts and attempts form part of the defence's arguments that what happened between Mu and his cousin was not manslaughter or any other crime; rather, it was 'her own sexual activity involving hanging and asphyxiation or [she] took her own life' (*R* v. *Mu*, 2014, p. 3). In short, she did it to herself.

Just as we saw in the context of evidencing consent, other vulnerabilities of women engaged in BDSM activity are also mobilised here. We have already seen how Dee has significant mental health challenges. We also hear that she became isolated:

> Dee had become very lonely about six weeks before the incidents with which you are concerned and [her friend] told you she thought Dee was seeing random taxi drivers in order to earn money. (*R* v. *Mu*, 2014, p. 22)

In her loneliness, Dee takes to having sex with 'random' men for money. We note also the timeline which coincides with when the sexual relationship with Mu started. Socially isolated, her apparent sexual deviance is seen to thrive. We see a similar narrative in Gaskell's case. Gaskell met his victim, Huteson, at a vulnerable point in her life:

> Laura Huteson was a much-loved daughter. Her mother has spoken in her statement movingly. She was aged 21 when you killed her. You were aged 24 at the time. It is a sad feature of this case that Laura Huteson had become estranged from her family. It is also a sad feature of this case that she ever became involved with you. (*R* v. *Gaskell*, 2018, p. 27)

She too, was estranged from her family, and in this enhanced state of vulnerability became involved with Gaskell. For both Huteson and Dee, the narratives about their precarious circumstances act, alongside representations of mental health issues, as threads which tie them, and their interest in BDSM, to pathologies of character that we see in the cultural representation of BDSM in the mainstream. The type of person who participates in BDSM – not a sex game gone wrong, not simply rough sex, nothing BDSM-adjacent – holds characteristics which are stereotypically flawed (promiscuous, drunk) folding into narratives of BDSM practitioners as damaged and perverse, and they do so because of the history of trauma, isolation and pain with which they live.

THE SPECTACLE OF BONDAGE

The interplay between BDSM as a subcultural practice and BDSM as it appears in the mainstream is becoming an increasingly observable phenomenon (Weiss, 2006). We see it in representations of BDSM in more mundane spaces (TV series, advertising), we see it in the proliferation of erotica that was also inspired by the *Fifty Shades of Grey* trilogy, we see it in how BDSM advice and information can be found in spaces that are not simply designated as kinky spaces; beyond the sex club, dungeon or euphemistically named 'adult store'. We find advice about BDSM at sexual health events on university campuses, in mainstream magazines and on health blogs. This means, of course, that the acts that BDSM comprises are more well known. People will expect that it involves bondage, biting, whipping, slapping, spanking, maybe name-calling, maybe role play (Herbernick et al., 2021). As we see in the accounts of what Pi, Lambda and Gamma got up to with the women who went on to accuse them, the power dynamic of submissive/dominant is understood, and in these – and all of the cases that are analysed in this book – the submissive role is feminine, the male role, dominant. The conduct, the vernacular ('be a good slave', 'Yes sir') and the practice of negotiating limits are all elements which are intrinsic to a BDSM subculture and which hold a coherence within the mainstream space of the courtroom. We saw, in the cases of Gamma, Gaskell and Pi, that the function of a safe word is logical within a court setting. Yet, in Gaskell, we also saw how the operation of a safe word could be misinterpreted as an attempt to mitigate the risks of BDSM rather than an indicator that the safe word is not being taken seriously. This is a spectacularisation of the safe word. Its concept is understood, it holds logic in descriptions of what happened in these encounters, but its deeper function, the obligations, mitigation, complexities and politics of the safe word, are but poorly and partially rendered. These elements remain legible in this space, notwithstanding that they are a mainstream spectacularisation of a subcultural practice.

It is in the accounts of who does BDSM and why they do it that we see this sexual subculture appear as spectacle more potently. As we have seen, mainstream representations of BDSM glorify some elements of the practice (what we do), with the aesthetic of the clothes, the equipment, the bondage (Sundén, 2023), but they also rely heavily on tropes heralding, from Krafft-Ebing and sexologists and psychoanalysts after him, that people who willing engage in this practice are in some way flawed. Spectacularised, BDSM is detached from its subcultural roots. Accoutrements of BDSM appear in these cases – the pathology, the language, the concept of limits – but they slide around only a superficial commodification of BDSM.

The case of Mu is particularly indicative of this pathologisation: suffering mental health issues, being lonely, being a drug user, being a sex worker, being 'sex mad', the presentation of Dee's background and personality are an object lesson in this pathologisation. The cases of Lambda and of Pi say nothing about why Aye and Bee were such enthusiastic submissives, though it is clear that, until it went wrong, they were both keen agents in these encounters. But in cases where some account of why people do this is offered, it is pathologised deviance that is given as the answer. It is the women whose vulnerabilities are used to explain their willingness to engage in BDSM. We do not know why Gaskell likes to use a knife to simulate threat during sex. Is he drug addicted? The victim of abuse as a child? Was he lonely? We are only told that it is Huteson who is all alone, estranged from her family. Why does Gamma like to pick up women off the street whom he does not know to take back to a house to have kinky sex with them? We do not know. We know only that it is because Enn is suicidal that she goes with him.

Hence, not only is the pathologisation of BDSM desire spectacularised in some of these cases, but that pathology resides in the bodies and acts of the women. Not with the men who willingly engage them in – drive, even – these encounters. This partial renderings of BDSM practice and practitioners means that notwithstanding greater awareness of what BDSM is and is not, that understanding can only ever be incomplete (Sheff, 2021). A consequence of that is the ease with which a spectacularised BDSM becomes a pathologised BDSM, quite distanced from the BDSM that people who practice BDSM would recognise (Weinberg et al., 1984). The pathologisation of those who practice BDSM endures, and the rendering of practitioners as broken, perverted, sad continues to resonate. As we will come to see, these abound with victim-blaming rape myths that nurture and sustain rape culture.

5. Spectacular Sex Positivity

The increase in cases where women have been killed or injured by men during a sexual encounter over the past twenty years is clearly observable, and it is telling us something about a changing sexual landscape. As I have outlined over previous chapters, this increase in cases where consent is offered as mitigation in court is accompanied by an increase in the accessibility and affordability of pornography and heightened presence of BDSM imagery and awareness of kink as a practice in the mainstream.

Mirroring, perhaps, the so-called 'sex wars' of the last century, arguments for or against the legal legitimacy of consent claims in BDSM practices where harms caused are more than 'transient or trifling', abound. Talking about non-normative sexual practice more, doing it more, it taking up more space within the mainstream imaginary, herald perhaps more acceptance of the practice. Or, perhaps more readiness to accept that there are people who do it, and these people are not necessarily pathological in their sexual desires: 'simply indulging in sadomasochistic sex doesn't necessarily involve a criminal act', the judge in the case of *Gaskell* reminds us (2018, p. 4).

This shift in perspective, from one which demonises BDSM as an 'evil thing' (*R* v. *Brown*, 1993, p. 9) to one which accommodates sadomasochistic desire as a possibility, might mark a transition in how sexuality is encountered in the courtroom: 'I am sure that Natalie's motivation arose from the fact that she derived sexual satisfaction by being beaten quite hard (*R* v. *Broadhurst*, 2018, p. 2). Is this an openness to sexual difference? Are we witnessing a softening of moral imperatives of how to do sex properly? Or, how to hold sexual desires that are correct? Does this mark a sex positive turn?

NEGATIVE/POSITIVE SEXUAL PRACTICE

It will come as no surprise that, and as we have already seen, in the main, sexual practice and non-normative sexuality in general have been encountered from a significantly negative – arguably moralistic – perspective in socio-legal contexts.

For example, up until the second half of the last century in England and Wales, male homosexual sex was criminalised, and even after it was decriminalised, this was only for sex which took place in specific places and in specific circumstances. This decriminalisation did not extend to Scotland and did not extend to personnel in the military until decades later. Low – almost non-existent – rape conviction rates in England and Wales are also an indicator of the problematic qualities of contemporary legal instruments. The specific ways that sex crimes are treated within the criminal justice system are an expression of sexual exceptionalism which 'treat sex differently from other activities' (Rothman, 2012, p. 119). In treating them differently, sex crimes are harder to secure convictions for. Sex offenders are more stigmatised and treated more punitively than offenders of different offences against another's body (Appleton, 2021, pp. 11–12) or are not punished at all. After all, it was not until 1991 in England and Wales, and 1993 in the USA, that marital rape was recognised as a crime in the first place.

Sexual expression – especially non-normative sexual expression – has been poorly understood and superficially engaged with in criminal cases (Sheff, 2021). The notion that desire or pleasure might be enough to justify the legitimacy of certain types of sex garners little traction. Sex is cast as dangerous where that danger is one that should never be confronted. Heteronormative, imperialist, moralistic measures are used to determine the difference between 'good' and 'bad' sex (Rubin, 2002 [1984]; Franke, 2001). Yet, as we will see in some of the discourses expressed within the cases analysed in this chapter, increasingly, space is held for the legitimate expression of non-normative sexual desire, including BDSM. What might this tell us about attitudes to non-normative sexual practice?

As I started to intimate in Chapter 2, the sex positivity movement emerges in dialogue with the feminist anti-porn movement. The principles which underpin sex positivity have been explored in a number of ways. Sex positive approaches generally consider that sexual practice and sexual pleasure in particular are important (Kaplan, 2014). Sex, according to Charlie Glickman (2000, p. 2), is neither good nor bad in this framework, but rather is a subjective practice with which we should try to have a better relationship. Glickman, like Margot Kaplan, and more recently Aimee Wodda and Vanessa R. Panfil (2020), has recognised that in the post-industrialist global north, sex has historically been viewed as something risky, shameful and problematic; as something to be controlled and discouraged other than when it takes place for procreative purposes (see also Rubin, 2002 [1984]). These principles might be described as sex negative ones, and so sex positivity can also be defined against sex negativity: as its opposite. Principles of openness, peacefulness and communication also nurture sex positive approaches (Williams et al., 2013; Wodda & Panfil, 2021).

Sex positive sex is informed, consensual, non-judgemental, and seeks to minimise any harm (Ivanski & Kohut, 2017). Sex can be refused with the same ease that it might be accepted within a sex positive framework. It is not compulsory. But where it happens, sex positive approaches are tolerant, respect diversity, are inclusive and accepting of difference (Williams et al., 2013; Ivanski & Kuhut, 2017). Significantly, sex positivity can be framed as anti-heteronormative in its attempts to centralise pleasure. It moves away from patriarchal figurations of sexual practice and could be an expression of the feminist pro-sex politics that engender it.

However, as Elisa Glick (2000) also demonstrates, thinking around sex positivity can also veer us towards a utopian ideal of emancipation through sex. Though sex is neither 'good nor bad' within a sex positive framework (Glickman, 2000), sex does matter. This focus on sex-as-freedom individualises sexual politics and divorces sexuality and sexual practice from the context in which it happens, who is doing it, and what the materiality of the conditions of the sex are like. Sex positivity can be spectacularised, and like consent, can enchant us into thinking that what we are doing is right, because we are so sex positive about it. In this commodified guise, sex positivity becomes a commodity; one which risks making sex compulsory and which renders refusals to have sex, or to have certain types of sex differently, deviant: prudish, uptight, frigid. So-called sex positive approaches foster hyper-sexualisation and silence the analysis of sexualised pathologies (Ivanski & Kohut, 2017, p. 223). It is spectacularised sex positivity that fuels the 'myth of everyday kink' which posits that everybody has kinky sex, now, and that non-normative sexual practices are a compulsory part of heterosexy sexual expression (Dobson, 2011; Gavey, 2024).

In a critical account of how sex positivity is weaponised, Jayne Swift (2021, p. 593) suggests that stigmatised sexual practices such as sex work (and we could add BDSM) are afforded a veneer of respectability through sex positive configurations (the 'happy whore', for Swift, who is college educated, white, able bodied, attractive, young (but not too young)). Respectability, as a counterpoint to that which is immoral, abject, or beyond the pale, becomes a rebuke to sex negativity which casts non-normative sexual expressions as abhorrent. Yet, in so doing, this sex positivity recruits stigmatised practices into a conservative, legitimated logic. In the context of sex workers, not all 'whores' get to be 'happy'. That construct is one that is aged, raced, classed, ableist and available only to certain bodies. Sex positivity, here, is used to foreground only the sex worker who does not conform to stereotypes of sex work. In this figuration, sex work might be a choice amongst many, the women might be highly educated, the sex work becomes a resistance to patriarchy. This is sex positivity which does not accommodate the drug addicted, the trafficked, the disabled, the destitute, those whose sex work they must be saved from. Sex positivity can thus be mobilised to erect borders between who is respectable and who is not.

This distorted idealisation of sex as always the 'right thing to do' transforms certain visions of sex positivity into ones which are as politically problematic and oppressive as are the sex negative structures that they posit to counter. Breanne Fahs (2014) notes how imperatives to be sexy, to orgasm with ease, to be sexually adventurous, risk obfuscating the different ways that the positivity becomes compulsory, to the erasure of desire. For Fahs, sex positivity must also accommodate the freedom to say 'no', or rather, 'maybe' (2014, p. 283). The 'politics of maybe', or what I have called the negative positivity, urges us to approach positivity critically, to attend to intersectionality – who has access to 'yes' and 'no'? And what price does this call to empowerment cost? In this way, we might approach these different strands of thinking about sex positivity as a heteroglossia of sex positivities where the impact, or multiplicities, of what sex positivity does is affected by the way it is mobilised, and the ends to which it might be used.

It is against this background of sex positive suspicion that I turn attention to how sex positivity and sex negativity emerge in some of these cases.

SOUPÇONS OF SEX POSITIVITY?

Why would women or men desire BDSM or BDSM-adjacent practices? In part, one answer is pleasure. As the judge in the case of *Tenniswood* (2016, p. 4) tells us, the 'squeezing [of the victim's neck] during consensual sexual intercourse [is supposed] to heighten her enjoyment'. People do it because they like it. Despite some scholarship telling us that women do not obtain pleasure from asphyxiation in sex, clearly, some might (see Edwards, 2015). Pleasure and desire, are, as Katherine M. Franke and Kaplan both note, largely absent from discourse about sexual practices in legal commentary. That something is pleasurable, wanted, erotic, *even if it is also risky or dangerous*, is not a good enough reason to accommodate it as something that can be consented to in law. We saw this in discussions of consent in Chapter 3. Here, when we think about pleasure, I suggest that we can think of it as an indicator of the influence of sex positivity on legal discourse. Pleasure can be understood as subjective, fluid, varied. Pleasure is usually enjoyable (Kaplan, 2014, p. 94). Yet, pleasure is not straightforwardly 'nice'. We can experience pleasure in activities and experiences that are also dangerous. Sometimes they can be pleasurable because they are dangerous. Autoerotic asphyxia is enjoyable, one summing up tells us, because 'starving the brain of oxygen ... is supposed to heighten the sexual pleasure of the person who is asphyxiated' (*R* v. *Foster*, 2018, p. 43). Debby Herbernick et al. (2022) remind us, in their study of women who engage in sexual asphyxia, that women can find things both scary and exciting and want to engage with them for that reason.

Yet, 'pleasure is not currently recognised in law as a major life activity' (Franke, 2001, p. 208). Pleasure, especially women's pleasure, is not part of the construction of sexual citizenship through legal discourse. The rendering of female ejaculation as obscene when it appears in pornography, where male ejaculation is not, is an example of this. The erasure of feminine masochistic desires that we saw in Chapter 4, in which women who fantasise about 'men dominating them' are framed as having 'internalised passivity' rather than as expressing what might be an authentic, deeply held desire, is another (Fahs, 2014, p. 281).

The ongoing criminalisation of BDSM is an expression of sex negativity, as is the construction of pleasure in sexual encounters as 'less valuable' than pleasure acquired from other risky activities that people engage in for leisure, such as American football, wrestling, boxing or Mixed Martial Arts (Kaplan, 2014, p. 123). These expressions of sex negativity are also expressions of sexual exceptionalism, where the sexualised elements of pleasure renders it more dangerous, and perhaps less moral than non-sexual practice (Wodda & Panfil, 2020). Would sex positivity be able to recruit BDSM back into respectability? Is this what is going on in some of these cases?

We have already encountered the case of Mu in Chapters 3 and 4. Mu was found not guilty of the manslaughter of his cousin, Dee, who was discovered hanging by her neck on her bed. He was asleep next to her. They been involved in a sexual relationship that was accompanied by exchanges of explicit sexual text messages in which they detailed graphic, sexually aggressive acts that they wanted to participate in with each other:

> 'Gonna tie you up for a couple of days next time I come up. I beat you, burn you, fuck you daft, then give you my knob in your mouth until you pass out'
> 'Is your cock hard and throbbing for me? It gonna get me some of what I like'
> 'Gonna singe your nipples and cunt while you tied up till you beg to be fucked'

> 'I will suck you knob and then beg you all night to fuck me just so I can buzz off the burning' (*R* v. *Mu*, 2014, pp. 25–6)

Mu's defence explained that the messages were 'just text talk' that he wrote whilst drinking alcohol. He had no interest in BDSM and BDSM-like sex and never practised this with Dee. They would usually have what he called 'normal' sex and take drugs together. The court heard that what happened to Dee she did to herself; she was suicidal; she was a sex worker; he was asleep when it happened. Dee, remember, was 'sex mad' (*R* v. *Mu*, 2014, p. 22).

In their summing up, the judge reminded the jury that:

> There is, I am sure you would agree, a mosaic of sexual preferences among all adults and it really is not a matter for other adults to pass judgement on such matters in a court. The law does not concern itself with sexual preferences or morality or any emotions connected with all of that. Put morality and views about sexual preferences to one side in this case. (*R* v. *Mu*, 2014, p. 5)

> What people do in the privacy of their own homes, and providing there is consent, is, you may feel, entirely a matter for them. The law is not concerned with sexual preferences, or the way people wish to lead their lives. That is for them in a free society ...
>
> None of us is here to sit in judgement about morality and lifestyles. We all live our lives the way we wish. The law is here to seek to protect individuals, not govern morality. We live in much more sexually liberated times than previous generations. (*R* v. *Mu*, 2014, pp. 6–7)

This lengthy explication of toleration of difference and openness to sexual diversity without judgement clearly chimes with the sex positive narratives identified by Williams et al. (2013) Wodda and Panfil (2020, 2021), above.

Consent appears as a key part, not just of BDSM and BDSM-adjacent activity, but also of sex positivity more broadly (Pitagora, 2013; Ivanski & Kohut, 2017; Galilee-Belfer, 2020). Such a move also makes clear that libertarian principles of individualised choice, self-determination and privacy are guiding principles which underpin this expression of openness to sexual difference (Fanghanel, 2020). Indeed, what we see at play here are similar principles of the 'privacy of [the] home' as those which informed the influential case of *R* v. *Wilson* (1996) that we encountered in Chapter 2, in which a consent defence was available to a man for branding his initials onto his wife's buttocks. The judge makes clear the link between a tolerance for the 'mosaic of sexual preferences' and existing in more 'sexually liberated times' which, on the one hand, works to normalise the possibility of non-normative sexual practice whilst, on the other, also linking this to a temporalised cultural shift;

before, we were not sexually liberated, and now we are. Having established a principle of non-moralising tolerance that echoes with sex positive principles and that is intended to encourage the jury to also approach their judgment with a sex positive frame of mind, the judgment continues to further outline elements of the case.

Referring to the significant number of text messages exchanged between Mu and Dee, some of which you have already seen in this chapter, the judge asks:

> Does it give an indication, if you needed any further indication, of what she liked, but from his viewpoint does it give an indication of what he liked or was it, as he asserts to you, drunken sex chat via text? (*R* v. *Mu*, 2014, p. 28)

Text message conversations between Mu and Dee were relayed to the court at length. The content and tone of the messages was explicitly sexual and explicitly about sexual activity which incorporated a sadomasochistic element to it. Indeed, the judge is unequivocal about Dee's interest in sadomasochistic sex. The conversations between the two demonstrate what appears to be an enthusiastic back and forth exchange about their plans together when they would meet. For Mu, it was just 'drunken sex chat', as the judge explains here, and this formed part of Mu's defence.

Whilst Dee's contribution to the exchange is taken as evidence 'if [the jury] needed any further indication' of her desire for sexual practice which eroticises violence, for Mu – just as much of a participant in the message exchange as she – could it be more innocent? Though this statement does suggest openness to the possibility that Dee may enjoy and desire the sadomasochistic encounters that she describes, the judge rhetorically wonders whether 'any further' indication of her desires were 'needed'. Dee's desire becomes figured as excessive. And her excessive desire is one-sided and directed towards an array of men with whom she had had sexual relationships. Excessive desire and the presentation of women as hypersexualised is a victim-blaming trope which folds into contemporary myths about the culpability of lascivious women for any harm that befalls them. The judgment continues:

> She plainly acted as, at least, a part-time prostitute. He had no problem with that conduct. (*R* v. *Mu*, 2014, p. 18)

Her sex work is offered here not to explain what might have happened between Mu and Dee and how she died, but to paint a picture of Dee and the sort of relationship that she had with Mu. Sex work – or 'prostitution' as it is called here – remains a stigmatised practice. The mention of sex work which is not relevant to the events that lead to Dee's death operates against this stigma to further cast her as morally problematic, as someone promiscuous, and as someone who through this promiscuity might, in part, be culpable for her own sex-related death.

We see this iterated in comments made by the judge about the presence of semen from 'another person' – 'impossible to say who' – in her vagina (*R* v. *Mu*, 2014, p. 5). Though Dee was having sex with Mu alone at the time that she died, the evidential fact of her promiscuity through the presence of unknown semen in her anus and vulva is presented to the jury and acts as evidence of the practices that Dee engaged in. A sex positive reading of Dee's sex work would understand it as mere work that was, to paraphrase Glickman (2000) 'neither good nor bad', and the fact that she was having consensual sexual intercourse with different people within the same short period as a matter of personal choice that was also 'neither good nor bad' and that was also manifestly irrelevant to the fact of her death. Indeed, the relevancy of semen of different men (insofar as it can be relevant) might only be in the way that it plays on normative (and sex negative) morality about promiscuous sex. The judge's framing of the facts of this case in the summing up upholds, on the one hand, the possibility of sex positivity as a guiding principle whilst also relying on sex negative, rape myths endorsing discourse on the other. Though this is 'not a court of morals', we can see moralising which condemns non-normative sexual expression entering by the back door.

This conflicted dichotomy, also emerges in the way that Charlotte Teeling is spoken about in the case of *Bailey*. We encountered this case in Chapter 3. In February 2018, Teeling met Richard Bailey. CCTV shows them kissing, holding hands, and buying drugs and alcohol before going back to his flat where they had consensual sex together and watched pornography on her phone. As they were having sex, he was strangling her neck, apparently at her behest, and she died. He said it was an accident and that he did not mean to kill her. He said everything that he did with Teeling was in response to her requests. He was found guilty of murder. At the beginning of their summing up, the judge tries to set the scene:

> This is not a court of morals. I strongly suspect that, in these days, it no longer needs to be said. Many years ago, people would have taken a view one way or another about two people meeting up and going and having intercourse within such a very short space of time. People would take a view about people looking at pornography and all that sort of thing. I doubt very much if a modern jury would be remotely moralistic about any of that but, just in case you were tempted, please don't be. (*R* v. *Bailey*, 2018, p. 16)

In this case where Teeling died during a consensual sexual encounter with Bailey, we hear the judge remind the jury that they should not consider with opprobrium (or more euphemistically, perhaps, 'take a view' about) the actions of people who have sex with each other immediately after meeting. As in the case of Mu, the statement appears to leave open the possibility for tolerance, or openness to sexual practices that the jury themselves might not agree with.

These views also resonate with the tolerance and acceptance of difference that are held within sex positive approaches (Glickman, 2000). We have seen that the principle of accepting diversity is a key tenet of sex positive narratives. Pornography is also considered to be morally problematic in the mainstream, so the emphasis on not 'taking a view' on the use of it also appears to work towards this. The case concerns Bailey, in which he, not Teeling, is on trial. The suggestion that the jury should not 'take a view' on 'two people meeting up and going and having intercourse within such a very short space of time' leaves open the possibility that it is *also Teeling* upon whom 'a view' may be taken, opening up the possibility that she might be held in some way responsible for what happened to her, and discursively reinforcing the additional burden that women carry in sexual encounters.

This reflects the possibility that the jury may be less apparently sex positive than the judge, but also discursively reinforces that this would, if not guarded against, be an understandable position to hold. Indeed, in guarding against 'taking a view', the judge's language here, normalises 'view taking'; the idea that it is normal to be critical of people who watch pornography and have intercourse without knowing each other, but that (and borrowing from Rubin, 2002 [1984]), though it is 'tempting' to stay in the charmed middle, the jury must not cast Bailey and Teeling's behaviour into the outer limits.

Alongside this, and before giving this sex positive advice to the jury, the judge reminds the jury of the following information:

> We need to think about the agreed fact that came late in the day but is an agreed fact about her activities as a webcam girl. Now, why do you know about that? … it helps you perhaps from two points of view. One is the question of anal intercourse … You will remember that what Mr Bailey said to the police was it wasn't actually his wish or her instigation that anal intercourse took place. He said it was a mistake and that he was surprised by how easy intercourse was and, from that point of view, it may plainly be of relevance to know that she acting as a webcam girl filmed herself inserting a sex toy into her anus on several occasions. (*R* v. *Bailey*, 2018, pp. 2–3)

Teeling died of manual strangulation during a sexual encounter with Bailey. The statement here about anal penetration is presented as something that may 'plainly be of relevance' to the jury when ascertaining whether or not anal penetration was deliberate or not. But how far *is* this really relevant? Bailey was not charged with rape, so the question of whether or not anal sex happened with his or her consent does not need to arise. It should be noted, and the judge is explicit about this in the preceding paragraph, that the question of whether Teeling consented to sex is not one that is posed to the jury. Anal intercourse, whether wanted or not, was not what caused the death of Teeling. This statement about the 'ease' with which anal intercourse was possible emerges against a cultural context in which heterosexual anal intercourse remains taboo, stigmatised, or, indeed is considered to be 'trashy' (Benson et al., 2019, p. 201). Drawing attention to both the anal intercourse and the fact that it is was 'surprising' and 'easy' works to paint Teeling as sexually improper and promiscuous. Moreover, that on several occasions Teeling would penetrate her own anus as part of online sex work is also presented as 'plainly of relevance', makes her sex work relevant to the interaction between she and Bailey despite the fact that their encounter was not one that took place within the context of sex work.

As with Dee, the stigma of sex work contributes to a demonisation of Teeling, whose promiscuity is used to paint a picture of who she was, quite apart from whether the webcamming or the anal penetration had any bearing on her death. This form of victim blaming is laced with sex negativity. Drawing attention to denigrated practices like anal sex or sex work as acts which are noteworthy, or somehow explanatory, reinforces their non-normative and stigmatised status. They suggest an intolerance of these practices, or at least a lack of acceptance that these practices might be unexceptional and unblameworthy. The conjunction of the incitement to tolerance, coupled with the evidence of non-normative and stigmatised sexual practices, troubles the potential of sex positive approaches here.

We see this unfold in a different way in the case of Jason Gaskell, who we also encountered in Chapters 3 and 4. On 27 February 2018, Laura Huteson was stabbed in the neck by Jason Gaskell as part of a so-called consensual sex game gone wrong. Gaskell pleaded guilty to gross negligence manslaughter and was sentenced to six years in prison. As part of his defence, he explained that knife play was part of his routine sexual activity, and he did not intend to harm Huteson. The couple had met each other only a few hours earlier that day. The significance of the guilty plea in this case is that any claim of her consent is used to mitigate the sentence rather than being used as evidence of his potential innocence.

The acts that led to Huteson's death – stabbing in the neck – occurred as part of consensual knife play. The consent element of the knife play is not, at any point, called into question during this sentencing remark, but is rather taken at face value, as we saw in Chapter 3. Knife play is a high-risk, but well-known, BDSM activity that involves the simulation of cutting or teasing and scraping the skin with the knife blade to enhance the sexual experience. The judge explains:

> Judge: – because it is – simply indulging in sadomasochistic sex doesn't necessarily involve a criminal act—
> Prosecution: No.
> Judge: – but here, where you've got the knife involved, it's grossly dangerous.
> Prosecution: Yes. It may be one of those hybrid-type cases. Holding a knife to somebody throat is – is an unlawful act potentially. But where she consents to that—
> Judge: Well, I think you can consent to that because you're not actually being physically hurt.
> Prosecution: No.
> Judge: It – it's simulated threat. This isn't a real threat. (*R* v. *Gaskell*, 2018, p. 3)

The judge in this case is not trying to help a jury determine guilt. Guilt has already been assumed by Gaskell himself. He is trying to grapple with the complexities of accommodating sadomasochistic desire with the law. Holding space for Gaskell's sexual interest in knife play does look like an accommodation of difference:

> Judge: he didn't have this knife for any conventional criminal purpose. He had it to enhance, in curious ways, sexual gratification.
> Prosecution: Yes.
> Judge: It wasn't being used for an unlawful purpose. I mean, I don't doubt for one moment that in this bizarre form of roleplay they were – he was threatening but it's not genuine threats.
> Prosecution: Not – not at all.
> Judge: It's – it's simulated threats for the purposes of a sexual act.
> Prosecution: Exactly, and that's why, and as your Lordship has quite properly observed, that idea of the safe word, which may not mean – mean much to a lot of people, but in their environment it – it provides a safety net of sorts. (*R* v. *Gaskell*, 2018, p. 14)

Indeed, engaging, as we saw in Chapter 4, with norms of BDSM, such as safe words and their function, marks a step towards understanding that different expressions of sexual practice can be equally valid (Williams et al., 2013). Yet, here too, the judge's comments hold onto the balancing act between acceptance and denigration. The sexual gratification Gaskell that gets from knife play is 'curious' and 'bizarre'. It is still held outside of sexual conduct that is OK.

Desire and pleasure are core principles of sex positive approaches. Acknowledging desire and its complexity, centring pleasure as a legitimate sexual aim opens up understanding of sexual practice to a fuller accommodation of what sexual practice might harness. These can be intersectional, non-heteronormative, non-genital centric: anything. Yet, when pleasure and desire appear in these accounts of BDSM and BDSM-adjacent practices, they are mobilised against women, who are also the victims in these encounters.

The case of Ashley Foster concerns the murder of Megan Bills. Foster strangled Bills and then hid her body in his wardrobe. Her body was only discovered a couple of weeks later by staff who worked in the hostel that Foster was living in. Bills was seventeen years old when she died. Foster was found guilty of murder. In his account, however, we hear that swiftly after meeting Foster, Bills had:

> gone into Foster's room and he [the neighbour] could hear the sounds of them having sex. He said he heard Foster grunting – this is your agreed fact – and she sounds like she was enjoying it very loudly. (*R* v. *Foster*, 2018, p. 27)

Elsewhere, in his evidence, Foster explains that:

> She tells me she likes to be strangled, so I oblige her, I strangled her, and she loved it so much she comes … over me and then as I released her, her eyes closed. I just thought she passed out from the orgasm, so I just left her on my bed, thinking she would be OK. (*R* v. *Foster*, 2018, p. 6)

As with Huteson, Bills, we are told, had become more promiscuous before she died. As with Dee, DNA evidence 'from her trousers' indicated that she had 'had a number of sexual partners' recently before her death and this, it is suggested, indicates that she was 'prepared to engage with Mr Foster in consensual sex when she had known him for just a few hours. She may have been willing to try something different' (*R* v. *Foster*, 2018, p. 9). The 'something different' here is choking during sex. We saw in the case of Dee and Teeling above, and in the cases of Lambda and Pi concerning consensual BDSM play, women's pleasure in, and desire for, BDSM and BDSM-adjacent activity holds space within a courtroom context yet here, that pleasure, those desires, are legitimate but are *also* offered up as the reason the women are killed or injured.

Orgasms are not often mentioned in the any of the cases that I have analysed here. Orgasms are considered to be expressions of pleasurable sexual encounters, though of course, encounters can be pleasurable without orgasm, and orgasm does not always mean that sex was pleasurable, or desired, or indeed consented to. There are a host of complex politics around the orgasm as object in sexual encounters (Vance, 1993). Within a heteronormative encounter, female orgasms are politicised both as an expression of female emancipation and as a 'marker of male prowess' (Fahs, 2014, p. 276). When Emily Thomas et al. (2017) analyse the phenomenon of women faking orgasm to make unwanted sex finish faster, they are pointing to the way in which female orgasms become affiliated to male sexual skill. They become co-opted into a performance of successful hetero-masculinity. In Foster's rendering, Bill's desire was so great, her orgasm so strong, that she 'came over' him and was rendered unconscious by this. Likewise, Edward Tenniswood wanted the court to know that he was 'not a selfish lover' in his encounter with India Chipchase, whom he went on to strangle to death.

> He came before she did but, because, he said, he's not a selfish lover, he wanted her to have an orgasm as well and he put one arm around her and manipulated her with his left hand until she achieved an orgasm. He described her as making an exhaling gasp and her body spasming. Now, that's relevant because that happened on the second occasion too, he said, which may well, you may think, be her actually dying and he said he mistook it for her orgasming again on the second occasion. (*R* v. *Tenniswood*, 2016, p. 19)

Again, female orgasms here propel Chipchase and Bills closer to death. Both Tenniswood and Foster interpret their gasps as expressions of pleasure, when they are instead potentially their final gasps for air (James Morton also stopped strangling Hannah Pearson when 'he heard her take a big gasp for air' (*R* v. *Morton*, 2017, p. 3)). Where male orgasms are mentioned, this is only in terms of failed orgasms – Mu 'could not ejaculate because of the drugs he was on' (*R* v. *Mu*, 2014, p. 23), Coates could not get an erection because Banner 'could not get [him] hard]' (*R* v. *Coates*, 2012, p. 20) – or to note where the ejaculations happened (in the vagina, in the anus (*R* v. *Bailey*, 2018, p. 33), on the bed (*R* v. *Pi*, 2014, p. 10), in [her] hair, face, mouth (*R* v. *Gamma*, 2018, p. 36), female orgasm is offered up to demonstrate that the sexual encounter was wanted and was good. Holding space for the female orgasm resonates with the sex positive emphasis on pleasure (that is heteronormatively contingent on men). But this analysis helps us see precisely how easy it is for that expression of sexual pleasure to rehearse tropes that elide female sexual pleasure with danger, and in many of these instances, death (Fahs, 2014).

SPECTACLES OF SEX POSITIVITY

These cases demonstrate in different ways how sex positive discourses – especially those of tolerance, openness and non-judgement – appear to emerge in how they are described. What also appears to emerge is a sex positivity that is spectacularised. When something is spectacularised, it is, as we know, divorced from the object being looked at. The spectacle is the ultimate in commodity fetishism (Debord, 2021 [1967]). When something is spectacularised, it becomes hyperreal, meaning that it becomes detached from its originary referent, becoming merely a simulacrum of that origin (Baudrillard, 1994 [1981], p. 6). Here, the originary referent – the spectacularised object – is sex positivity.

As we also saw in the contexts of consent and BDSM in chapters before this one, it is a reified and reduced version of sex positivity that might be identified here. Where principles of sex positivity (acceptance of difference, that sexual expressions are valid, that desire is enough, focus on pleasure) are expressed, they are almost immediately erased by sex negative underpinnings that have characterised so much of how sexual practice is dealt with through a criminal justice lens (Appleton, 2021). We see this in the way that sex work, promiscuity and non-normative sexual practices are conjured and then dismissed as unseemly in the accounts given of the deaths of Dee, Keeling, Huteson and Bills. Though none of these women were killed because of their involvement in sex work or because they may have been promiscuous, offering up these details – details which are roundly situated as problematic and as on the outer limits of sexual practice – paints a picture which undermines the sex positive potential of guidance to the jury about sidelining their own preconceptions of acceptable sexual conduct. Indeed, we might even suggest that the foregrounding of sex positive messaging responds to a sex negative reality; that by expressing sex positive imperatives, the courts lay bare the dominance of sex negativity within courtroom spaces.

This imperative is all the more evidenced in the ways that the concepts of emancipation, freedom and choice – all sex positive concepts – become mobilised in courtroom contexts. The importance of self-determination, and of the right to choose, and to choose not to, rumble through sex positive accounts of what can be done to foster a more socially just world. And yet, the concerns about sex positivity that Glick (2000), Fahs (2014), Katherine Angel (2021) and Swift (2021) point to do emerge when sex positivity is spectacularised. When sex positivity is thought of just as an imperative to 'yes', when sex positivity is only available to some bodies and excludes others, when sex positivity is always-already raunchy, permissive and game, where sexual ambivalence, not-knowing and timidity are unavailable, the work that sex positivity might do is stymied.

Holding space for women to claim that they love sex, that they love BDSM or BDSM-adjacent sex, that they love sex with people that they have only just met, and holding the possibility of those as legitimate choices and desires is clearly an expression of sex positivity. Holding that space without shame and without condemnation, likewise, is sex positive. Accepting that whilst what you get up to might not be to my taste, you should be free to do it without harm, or risk of criminalisation within certain limits, is sex positive. And yet, as the cases here do show, the sex positivity that we see is contingent and spectacularised.

Yes, judges' comments encourage open-mindedness. They remind juries that they should approach these cases with tolerance, non-judgementally, and respectful of sexual desires and practices that they may not share, or even understand. They are reminded that they are 'not a court of morals', that it 'is not a matter for other adults to pass judgment' on the sexual preferences of others, that the use of 'safe words' (even when they are not responded to quickly) act as indicators of sound, responsible sadomasochistic play.

Alone, these instructions or comments would seem to indicate that there is a shift occurring in how some courts are prepared to understand non-normative sexual expression; that these desires might not be, intrinsically, on the outer limits (Rubin, 2002 [1984]). At the same time, we can see that this is an expression of sex positivity that is spectacularised, because in each case the judges' comments undermine the sexual agency and dignity of women who have died. By drawing on tropes that emphasise women's deviant sexual practice – their sex work, their use of sex toys, their sexual fantasies, their promiscuity – as constituent features that are relevant to their deaths, the limits of sex positive imaginaries become very clear.

Through spectacular sex positivity, the desires of these women are neoliberalised. They are cast as sexually emancipated, free to choose to participate in a diversity of sexual practice and responsible for their choices. This freedom comes at a price, though. It legitimises the 'she asked for it' response that campaign groups and researchers are so vocally critical of (Yardley, 2021; Edwards, 2015, 2023). It pays lip-service to an emancipated and pro-feminist juridical agenda without engaging with a cultural background which normalises violence against women. This version of sex positivity ignores the structural power imbalances that compose current so-called sex games gone wrong narratives (Yardley, 2021). It frames whatever happens within a sexual encounter as desired, consensual and straightforward without attending to the context in which these take place. Often people have been drinking alcohol or using drugs; often they do not know each other, and have not spent time discussing what they want, what they do not want, what their limits and safe words might be; often there is an age difference which disadvantages the victim and her capacity to speak up, ask for, or refuse what is happening. Spectacularised sex positive framings obscure the thorny aspects of sexual negotiation or sexual encounters that critics of sex positivity point to. Indeed, in these cases, sex positivity facilitates victim blaming and echoes, rather than undermines, rape myths which cast women who might be sex workers, promiscuous, or living complex lives as legitimate victims of violence and death occurring as part of a so-called sex game gone wrong, or sadomasochistic encounter that they have asked for.

WHAT COULD A SEX POSITIVE JUSTICE ENCOUNTER LOOK LIKE?

It is clear that certain imaginations of sex positivity have emerged in criminal cases, where a non-normative sexual encounter appears to have occurred. However, as we have also seen, these are partial, incomplete, surficial expressions of sex positivity. Rape myths, which nurture rape culture, continue to proliferate. More than this, sex positive narratives themselves are put to work to bolster these rape myths through responsibilisation discourses which demonise, alienate and dehumanise women who have died during these encounters.

Yet, there does indeed remain a need for more consistent and committed engagement with sex positive principles, or negative positivity, in cases which involve sadomasochism or adjacent sexual practice. Doing this helps to achieve material justice for women, whether they practice BDSM or have falsely been figured as doing so.

One of the more interesting possibilities afforded by a sex positive framework is the capacity that some scholars find in transforming social justice through it. Both Williams et al. (2013) and Wodda and Panfil (2021) posit that sex positivity, when threaded through educative practices, for instance, helps to reduce inequalities. It nurtures minoritarian ways of understanding the world and works to decentre the dominance of majoritarian ways of knowing. *Contra* Glick's (2000) critique that mere transgression, or mere decentring is complacent in its aims, certain epistemological practices – or indeed praxes – of sex positivity can be put to work to foster better social justice outcomes. They might indeed 'engage with the political and economic contexts that most sex radicals recognise as oppressive' (Glick, 2000, p. 40). According to Williams et al. (2013), it is sex negativity which nurtures prejudice and fosters violence. It is sex positivity that offers some of the way out of this.

What might a sex positive criminal justice system look like? Wodda and Panfil (2021) have already done some work on this idea and posit that sex positive approaches might harness the potentialities of sex positive thought to critique dominant ways of thinking and acting at an institutional level. Recognising that institutions of power as well as *dispositifs* of belief systems, education, the role of the family, the role of the social realm, construct the sex negativity which prevails in contemporary social life, Wodda and Panfil (2021) suggest that sex positive approaches need to also intervene at an institutional and societal level, rather than an individual one.

A principle of sex positivity, as we have seen, is the acceptance of difference, or reaching across difference. This position, which is rooted in feminist praxis about how we orientate ourselves in our relationships with each other, builds on Maria Lugones's (1987) influential work on loving perception and world travelling. World travelling asks that we 'travel' to the worlds of our interlocuters, our critics, our friends, to try to better fathom how it is that they meet us in this encounter. What is their world like? This is accompanied by practising loving perception; seeing and affirming someone's whole humanity, even across difference. To see someone with love does not mean to agree with them, does not require you even to like them, but it is a call to encounter difference with openness, curiosity, and cognisant of our own pain, biases, worlds.

By reaching across difference through loving perception, the other does become less other. We become closer to them, we move to a position of understanding – which does not mean agreeing with them – and with compassion, come together in the encounter. Gayle Rubin's (1984) image of the wheel of sexual practice is one that I return to over and again because of the neat way in which the charmed circle and the outer limits interact with each other. Charmed sexual practices like heterosexuality, or sex with just one other person, are pinned in place by their opposite: homosexuality and group or solo sex. The tension between that which is in the centre and that which is not is tidily held in place by social norms, moralistic expectations and patriarchal heteronormativity.

Certainly, the opprobrium with which some sexual practices such as non-monogamy or non-reproductive sex, or, indeed, BDSM are met with now is different to the prejudice and discrimination that activists like Rubin would have encountered in the 1980s. There is more awareness of, and acceptance of, different ways to be a sexual citizen. Within the BDSM community, something like this world travelling might be referred to as 'your kink is not my kink but your kink is OK' (or, more snappily, YKINMKBYKIO), which essentially seeks to hold space for different desires without shame, and without compromising one's own sexual ethics. Yet, as we have also seen, sex negativity-fuelled shame, victim-blaming and violence still endure. Reaching across difference, with tools offered to us by some sex positive approaches, coupled with a praxis of loving perception, helps us to pierce Rubin's charmed circle of sexuality, so that a hierarchy of 'good' and 'bad' sex is less stable. Or rather, that we can turn our attention to sex that is not 'good' from an ethical perspective, and away from sex that is not 'good' from the perspective of normative moral framings.

Coupled with the principle of reaching across difference and world travelling is the notion of attending to the situatedness of who is speaking. This also requires encounters with compassion and understanding where people are speaking from. Consider, intersectionally, who is speaking? who can speak? As Swift (2021) demonstrated in the context of sex workers, sex positive approaches can sometimes only be available to bodies which conform to other normative positionalities of power delineated along axes of ethnicity, class, age, ability, or appearance, for instance. Situatedly-focused enquiries which take account of these intersections of power better enable everyone to speak, not simply those for whom sex positivity is already available. Becoming self-aware, in this way, also helps us to grapple with our own biases and shortcomings when it comes to encountering others. Trans-, homo-, whore-, kink-phobia are all normative (Sheff, 2021). Ageism, sexism, racism, ableism are too. A sex positive approach to sexual practice in legal settings (and, indeed, beyond these) would acknowledge this reality, enable us to see it in ourselves and begin the battle against these norms.

A theme that cuts through most accounts of the changes that sex positivism might foster is that of education. Most obviously, as highlighted by Wodda and Panfil (2021) and by Williams et al. (2013), sex positivity can be used to transform sexual education by resisting the appeal of shaming sex negative accounts within it. In the context of non-normative sexual practice and the law, Elisabeth Sheff (2021, p. 768) notes that training about BDSM subcultures can help legal practitioners become more familiar with the 'values and practices' of the subculture. Thus, they would become better able to distinguish between sexual practices which are consensual BDSM or

BDSM-adjacent, and intimate partner violence and abuse (Pitagora, 2013). For BDSM practitioners, and the BDSM curious, Sheff (2021) also recommends educative interventions in order to better understand the nuances of BDSM play, the risks, the safety measures that need to be taken and other practicalities. Through education, sex positive approaches can take aim at the institutional barriers which reinscribe sex negativity when sexual practices are interrogated in the courtroom.

Education, capacity-building, awareness-raising all help to demystify elements of BDSM practice, which, as we saw in Chapter 4, are misunderstood in non-BDSM contexts, such as, for instance, the courtroom. Education helps to elucidate different aspects of BDSM subculture. It helps to highlight subcultural norms such as the imperative to play sober (Sheff, 2021, p. 766), or to attend to consent negotiations (Williams et al., 2013), or to understand what safe words, or sub space, or hard and soft limits mean and look like. Sex positive education is made possible through accurate and de-stigmatised use of language (Glickman, 2000) and through dismantling the shame which upholds sex negative taboos. Sex positive education about non-normative sexual practice can begin the work of bringing about the socio-cultural change that we will need in order to become 'free of the myth of normality' (Glickman, 2000, p. 3).

WHAT WOULD A SEX POSITIVE JUSTICE ENCOUNTER DO?

The framing of sex positivity that I adopt here is not one that blithely believes that we can 'fuck our way to freedom' (Califia, 1988, p. 15). No thoughtful sex positive advocates think that sex is always the answer. As we see through Fahs's (2014) approach and through Glick's (2000) work, a 'sex as correct' attitude to sexual practice risks normalising the sexual availability and 'gameness' of one group of people for another, more powerful group (within a heteronormative encounter, women for men) on the one hand, whilst silencing or rendering 'other' perspectives which do not see sex as the answer. The negative positivity that I have posited here – or, as Fahs (2014, p. 283) puts it, the right to say 'maybe' – helps us to walk this line and to hold space for the plethora of voices about sex to speak and be heard.

I have noted in the context of education that sex positivity becomes possible through language. One thing that sex positivity enables us to do is to speak more thoughtfully about sexual offending and the way that sex offenders are treated in the criminal justice system (Williams et al., 2013, pp. 274–5). Sex offences are dreadful. Not all 'kinks' *are* 'OK'. And a sex positive framing of attitudes to sexual practice would better be able to engage with those desires or 'kinks' which are harmful, or which pose ethical problems, such as non-consensual sex, stares, touching, speech, or sex with those who cannot meaningfully consent (non-human animals, children, the dead; see Fischel, 2019). And yet, the way that sex offenders are treated within the criminal justice system is also dreadful. I have already pointed to the single-figure rape conviction rates that are endured in England and Wales. Where they are convicted, in some jurisdictions sex offenders are treated vastly differently to other offenders convicted of harassment or offences against the person (sometimes the need to be named on a register, sometimes restrictions on where they can live, or whom they can work with). This is, in part, because of sexual exceptionalism and taboos around sex crime which is an expression of sex negativity (Appleton, 2021).

A sex positive approach to sex crimes would take sex crimes seriously but would decouple these from disgrace and stigma which make these crimes hard to report, hard to convict and hard to be punished for. Sex positivity enables us to speak without shame, including forging the capacity to speak against power, to push against socio-cultural norms that are bigger than us, and to strive to bring about changes for a more social just world.

A sex positive approach which is fostered through world travelling, or through loving perception, or through reaching across difference is also one that is anti-racist, anti-essentialist and anti-heteronormative. Recognising the situatedness of human experience, impression, emotion and desire fosters the capacity to see beyond what it is that we already 'know'. This decentring of imperialist ways of knowing, this troubling of socio-cultural 'truths', empowers and encourages us to pursue understandings beyond the 'heterosexist and mono-normative' (Williams et al., 2013, p. 274). This does not mean that 'anything goes', or that openness to difference means that all differences are OK – we must hold on to our critical negativity amongst our positivity – but rather that we equip ourselves with the tools to start to do this work.

Joseph Fischel incites us to screw consent – to trouble what we mean by consent – and, rather than asking questions about consent, posit what it would mean to live what he calls a libidinally full life which facilitated human flourishing. Flourishing, following Martha Nussbaum (2011), recognises that the inherent dignity of the human condition must be acknowledged for people to live full and meaningful lives. We flourish when we can express ourselves autonomously when we have agency over our choices, when our conditions of life enable this flourishing. We flourish when our capacity, and right, to flourish is recognised by others. In French the word we would use for this is *épanouir*, which means to bloom, to unfurl, to open up. It is a word often used to describe a flower opening. Importantly, *épanouir* is a reflexive verb; it is something that you can only do to yourself. Etymologically, *épanouir* comes from the Old French term 'espanir' or 'espaner', meaning to expand, to take up space. Sex positivity can be a humanising philosophy that fosters a praxis which helps us to bloom. If sex negativity is like 'having an injury' (Glickman, 2000, p. 2), hobbling us, paining us, then opening up to positivity helps us to thrive in the fullness of our humanity. We can play, we can try, we can refuse, we can take risks, we can try again, we can explore, we can heal, we can try something else and something else again … sex positive approaches to justice encounters harbour the tools for us to take up space, and orient ourselves otherly, to achieve this human flourishing.

6. Consent and Instruments of Violence

> Since our sexuality has been for the most part constructed through social structures over which we have had no control, we all 'consent' to sexual desires and activities which are alienating to at least some degree. (Rian, 1982, p. 49)

> Sex alone can't liberate us, but in the mean time, it comforts us. Women want and need the freedom to be outrageous, out-of-doors, out-of-bounds, out after dark without being silenced or punished by stigma, forced reproduction, or murder. (Califia, 1988, p. 16)

Since I started writing this book in 2023, men and women have continued to be killed by men as part of so-called BDSM or BDSM-adjacent activity. Many more will have been injured. Some of these incidences will have been reported to the police, some will not have been. Some may have taken place amid the context of recognised BDSM, some will not have.

At the opening of this book, I posited that contemporary sexuality was both troubling, and in trouble. Some of the trouble that moved me to write this text was this ongoing antagonism between BDSM, the BDSM-adjacent and justice. How do we protect men and women who want to participate in BDSM without fear of criminalisation? How can we protect women and men who are killed or injured during sexual encounters whose consent is construed on their behalf, and without their voices? How can we do better when it comes to dealing with the murkiness of sexual practices, desires and cultures?

In this book, I have analysed cases where this antagonism plays out. These are cases that have come before the criminal courts because women have been killed or injured during a sexual encounter, and where the defendant's defence has sought to rely on the women's consent to mitigate his actions. I have posited that three themes are salient to understanding how these cases are presented in court and perceiving the discourses that they rely on to be socio-culturally legible. I posited that concepts about the complexity of consent, knowledge about BDSM subcultures and awareness of sex positive imperatives emerge in these cases. Whilst I have separated these themes out in order to make sense of them, it is clear that these slide over each other, too. The notion of consent, for instance, is so intrinsic to BDSM practice and what might be known about BDSM subcultures, and holding space for the possibility of consent in something that looks like a BDSM encounter is, in itself, a sex positive position to adopt. The cases that I have analysed across these themes can be used to tell different parts of the story about how BDSM and BDSM-adjacent practices became crucibles which fuel anxiety about sexuality. I have argued that this trouble is fuelled, in part, by the spectacularisation of consent, BDSM and sex positivity.

In this chapter, I want to bring these themes together to examine how they engage with, or enact, violence. From here I want to imagine how we can transform this impasse into a turning point which equips the contemporary social world to do better when it comes to sex.

THE PROBLEM OF VIOLENCE

As I have demonstrated across the past several pages, one of the problems with the way that sexual practices and desires are treated in legal contexts – particularly those which are non-normative desires and practices – emerges in the way that violence is figured as a normalising force which constructs contemporary sexual landscapes. Within an encounter which incorporates BDSM themes, the acts which might take place – restraint, flogging, spanking, biting – do look like aggressions, or acts of violence. People practicing BDSM might posit, conversely, that because these are violences that are wanted, they are not violence *tout court*. The distinction between violence and pleasure is important, as it is this distinction that makes the difference in the interpretation of the facts of the cases. As we saw in Chapter 2, the practices that the men in *Brown* engaged in were considered to be violences which 'breed cruelty'. They were distinguished from the consensual (indeed, instigated by her) branding of Janet Wilson in the 1996 case of *Wilson* because branding was considered to be a desirable adornment, unlike *Brown* which featured sadomasochism of 'the grossest kind' (*R* v. *Wilson*, 1997, p. 4). Here, violence and pleasure must always be held apart. Pleasurable violence cannot be sanctioned, believed in, accommodated or even desired.

There is the potential of a broader significance to this denial of pleasure as 'good enough'. Patrick Califia elegantly notes that 'if you live in a society that wishes you didn't exist, anything you do to make yourself happy disrupts attempts to wipe you out, or at the very least, make you invisible' (1988, p. 15). Califia is speaking in the context of lesbian sadomasochism, but the observations about injunctions against pleasure can be applied to sexual minorities and minoritised people beyond this. Imperatives to pleasure can be figured as a resistance to this erasure. The quashing of this pleasure is a violence.

The word violence stems etymologically from the Latin *violentia*, meaning force, or vehemence. Theorising violence, Hannah Arendt (2003 [1970]) posits that not only is violence always instrumental – a means to an end – but that is always non-consensual. From this vantage point, we can see how what goes on within a BDSM encounter begins to pose problems. The acts that take place, themselves, within a BDSM encounter do look like violence from the outside. Clearly, when women are killed during a sexual encounter, it is evident that violence that cannot be consented to has occurred. And yet, as the Law Commission in England and Wales themselves noted in 1995, violence which is non-fatal has a specific social meaning within BDSM subcultural contexts. To better understand BDSM would require adopting an emic approach which understands BDSM practice from the purview of the BDSM practitioners. Instead, from an etic perspective, commentators express sadness about what they hear from BDSM practitioners (*R* v. *Brown*, 1993; Hanna, 2001), they disbelieve that people really have desire for the practices (Edwards, 2015), or they consider that this desire is too dangerous, too much at risk of going wrong to be legitimated (Hanna, 2001; Herring, 2023). BDSM remains a risk to public health, to public morals and to society.

The violence that BDSM practitioners engage in then comes into conflict with violence as it is understood more broadly. If, as Arendt suggests, violence is instrumental, then for dominant male actors in the cases examined in this book, the sexual violence of men is an expression of virile, heteromasculinity; 'giving pain is simply a utility or side effect of man's aggressive sexual thirst' (Harris, 1982, p. 192). It is how they become men. Similarly, and echoing Krafft-Ebing, willingly receiving violence becomes an expression of subordinated femininity. None of this reckons with how practitioners themselves experience violence; as something that is wanted, as a sensation, as a different way of having a body that offers alternative pleasures.

I have also posited that the way BDSM and BDSM-adjacent practices are figured in these cases is also an expression of the contemporary sociocultural context in which they emerge. The tensions around whether or not what BDSM practitioners do is violent is one example of this. The criminalisation, in England and Wales and much of the global north, of BDSM practice which causes injury that is more than 'transient or trifling' is another. As has been noted by an array of scholars, the criminalising of this expression of sexual desire has manifest implications for the expression of autonomy and the forging of sexual citizenship (Cowan, 2010; Pa, 2001; Haley, 2015; Bradley, 2023), which are both intrinsic to the development of sexual justice. Creating these barriers becomes, in itself, a form of violence against practitioners within those subcultures.

It is important to hold on to the fact that whilst BDSM practitioners are in the minority, the criminalisation of much of BDSM practice becomes a symbolic problem, overall. It creates a silo which casts BDSM as always already deviant and always already other. This happens within a contemporary context where some aspects of BDSM have been co-opted into the mainstream and have been commodified, and against a background of contemporary rape culture. The criminalisation of BDSM then forms part of a constellation of sexual controls, normalisations and sanctions which compose that rape culture.

As I have demonstrated, the ways that consent discourses, BDSM and expressions of sex positivity are rehearsed reinscribes rape myths about masculinity, femininity and heterosexuality into the encounter. Figuring women who engage in non-normative sexual practice as victimisable because of their mental health issues (Gamma, Coates, Mu), their promiscuity (Mu, Gamma, Bailey, Gaskell, Pybus), their loneliness (Bailey, Tenniswood, Coates), or their age (Morton, Doblys, Foster) pathologises victims. Rape myths also fuel sex negative and victim-blaming and shaming discourses that emerged in the cases that have been encountered in this book. Rape myths work because they tell stories that we 'know' about sex. They rehearse stereotypes about appropriate masculinity and femininity; about who is a victim and who is a predator. Myths are timeless, meaning that they always exist in an ongoing everlasting present (Lévi-Strauss, 1955, p. 430). Because they become part of the enchanting banal backdrop of the everyday, they are hard to perceive and thus, hard to undo. Even when judges, in their summing ups, try to accommodate sexual difference, the ubiquity of rape myths penetrates their discourse. These rape myths are expressions of gendered, and gendering, violence.

THE PROBLEM OF STRUCTURAL VIOLENCE

Rape myths are violent – that much is evident – and they are expressions of a rape culture which normalises gendered violence, particularly against women. They also function in concert with structural violences. Here, the structures and systems which exert non-consensual force and vehemence on those who suffer under this violence are juridical ones (Arendt, 2003 [1970]).

It is an artefact of the methodology that I adopted to conduct this work that the voices of the women and men in each of these cases are ventriloquised by the words of the judge. Analysing the judge's summing up – which is intended to help and to guide the jury ahead of them deliberating in private – we clearly only hear the judge, and in nearly every case that I analysed the judge is at pains to remind the jury that the comments that the judge is making are about what he or she thinks is salient in the case. They do not purport to cover the whole of the case, or the evidence, and the jury is reminded each time that they must make their own decisions about what is helpful or not in their consideration of a case.

Analysing the words of the judge necessarily silences the voices of the victims. However, here are two elements to consider: in many of the cases I have analysed, the victim is silent anyway. They are not here to tell us what they wanted, what they agreed, what they intended. Mostly, we only have the defendants' word for it. Secondly, as incomplete as this summing up account may be, it is also how trials finish. The structure of the courtroom is unequivocally hierarchical. Roles and comportments are strictly codified. The hyper-civil conduct within the courtroom underpins principles of apparent neutrality, sobriety, control and obedience. The judge sits at the top of this hierarchical structure, with the jury as an adjunctive group who sit within this pyramid, as ultimate decision makers, but always under the guidance of the judge, who will have the final word.

Therefore, in the summing up of the case, the judge's instructions and notes for the jury take on a specific significance within the courtroom context. The judge's observations about what has taken place, who said what, to whom, when, and how, are intended to help the jury; not to persuade, not to influence, but to inform. As such, the voices expressed through the conduit of the judge will be influential, even if, holding this influence, the voices of the victims about consent are silenced, or at least only reported second hand.

The rigidity and the hierarchical structure of this juridical institution is one in which power also operates rigidly. Patriarchy, paternalism, ethnocentrism, class, heteronormativity and neoliberalism suffuse the discourses in the cases that I have examined here. We see them in squeamishness about non-normative sex, in condemnatory attitudes to sex work, in the reproduction of heteronormative romance or seduction scripts, in the demonising of promiscuity, in failures to, or refusals to, recognise the complexities of desire in sexual subcultures. We see them in the spectacularisation of consent, BDSM and sex positivity that are offered as ways to understand non-normative sexual practices.

CONSENT AS VIOLENCE

One of the more insidious ways that structural violence operates is in the way that it recruits consent as a weapon. Throughout this book, I have demonstrated how consent haunts the cases that have been analysed. In the cases of *Broadhurst* (2018), *Gaskell* (2018) and *Pybus* (2021) we have seen consent of the dead women used to mitigate, to defend the defendants' intentions, and to reduce the length of the sentence served for manslaughter by these men. We have seen in the cases of *Pi* (2014), *Lambda* (2013), *Gamma* (2018) and *Mu* (2014) that consent has been mobilised to exonerate defendants completely, even though, in the last of these cases one woman dies, and in two of the former three, women were left with bite marks, bruising and lacerations after their BDSM encounters; all of which might be considered to be more than transient or trifling.

Despite being convicted of murder, we saw in the cases of *Bailey* (2018), *Coates* (2012) and *Doblys* (2013) that the defendants were able to use notional concepts of consent as part of their defences. We see this, even though, as we know, and as is critiqued elsewhere, there is no consent defence in cases concerning sadomasochistic practice; much less that which results in the death of one of the parties.

We have also seen how approaches to understanding consent, BDSM and sex positivity are themselves spectacularised (Debord, 2021 [1967]). Their 'real' dynamics are concealed by partial representations, partial understandings, partial engagements with these phenomena. We have surficial expressions of consent, BDSM and sex positivism. They become, 'black boxed' (Latour, 1987). Black boxed concepts are ones that appear easy to use where that ease comes from a refusal (or inability) to interrogate how those concepts are made; what they comprise. Their murky complexity becomes obscured. The superficial ease with which they are invoked both hides and distorts their representations in these cases, and in discourses about sexuality beyond this. Indeed, what we encounter in these discourses is a hyper-real surface which uncritically misreads and mistakes these spectacles for reality.

In the context of consent, this idealism is particularly grave. As I have already suggested in the cases of *Gaskell*, *Pybus*, *Morton* and *Foster*, this black box of consent also falls into a black hole. We know there was consent because we know there was consent. Obviously circular, this logic betrays both how uninterested courts can be in what counts as consent and how powerful consent can be as an illocutionary act. In cases where consent has 'worked' as a defence (to exonerate men, to reduce their minimum tariff, to transform a murder charge into a conviction for manslaughter (Edwards, 2015)), it has been used to denigrate women. It has been used to moralise about their promiscuity, including sex work (*Mu*, *Bailey*, *Pybus*, *Foster*). It has been used to stigmatise them for their vulnerabilities, including mental health difficulties (*Tenniswood*, *Coates*, *Mu*, *Gaskell*, *Gamma*). It has been used to present women as debauched and sexually out of control – demanding their own sexual subordination (*Mu*, *Connors*, *Coats*, *Bailey*, *Pi*). In the cases of *Pi* and *Lambda*, where we hear from the women themselves about what they have unwillingly submitted to as part of deliberate BDSM practices, we are told that that they were jealous and acting out of spite because the men in the cases were in contact with other women. Consent is weaponised here in the way that it diminishes women – whether alive or dead – who have suffered in these cases. It paints them as sexually insatiable, sexually immoral, as manipulative, as liars, as women who put men in dangerous and risky situations; who can cause men harm (*R* v. *Gamma*, 2018, p. 42).

Consent is figured, as Joseph Fischel (2019) also notes, as a balm which absolves all ills. Its power to transform what people do to each other from illicit to licit acts enchants us. We know that consent is offered up as intrinsic to sexual encounters. We know the central importance that it holds within sexual subcultures. It is at the heart of educational practices around sexual conduct. Etymologically, a panacea (from the Greek 'pan' meaning 'all' and 'akes' meaning 'cure') *is* a black box *par excellence*. It does not invite us to consider what we talk about when we talk about consent. The mere presence of consent becomes enough. Constructing consent-as-panacea also becomes consent that is weaponised. It becomes an uninterrogatable alibi for sexual practice which has harmed. It exonerates these sexual violences, and, as we have seen, it eviscerates women in these cases, who, after all, are not on trial.

WOULD LEGALISATION OF A CONSENT DEFENCE HELP?

In England and Wales, where the cases analysed in this book have been tried, we know that there is no defence of consent to injury incurred for sexual gratification which is more than 'transient' or 'trifling'. This law, set out in *Brown*, has influenced Commonwealth and former Commonwealth jurisdictions around the world, including Australia, New Zealand and Canada.

The legal landscapes of BDSM are outlined in Chapter 2. For now, it serves to remind us that similar interdictions apply in many countries in Europe, in the USA, South Africa and India. Obscenity laws are used to criminalise some BDSM practice in other jurisdictions. In many jurisdictions, BDSM is not a sexual subcultural practice that can be engaged in without risk of criminalisation.

So, would a consent defence help? Would it have helped in the cases examined in this book, where tropes of BDSM are called upon to explain violence occurring within a sexual encounter? The debates for the right to raise a consent defence in a case comprising BDSM elements have been set out by various scholars on different sides of the question and are rehearsed in Chapter 2. They can be summarised thusly: on the one hand, pro-BDSM arguments posit that respect for the dignity and agency of BDSM practitioners and their sexual subjectivity should compel the creation of a consent defence. On the other hand, counter-discourses from scholars who are more sceptical about this posit that creating a defence of consent would be against public best interests, would be open to abuse, and is symbolically too close to intimate partner violence to be acceptable (Haley, 2015; Pa, 2001, Herring, 2023, Hanna, 2001).

I offer a more complex position. Should a consent defence be created? Should BDSM cases in which there is more than trivial injury be decriminalised? Yes, probably. But whether we are for or against the creation of a consent defence in BDSM cases, we can see that the current way that BDSM and the BDSM-adjacent is treated in the courts is problematic. We can see that it is a violence and it is an excuse for violence (Arendt, 2003 [1970]).

Why should this consent defence be created? Because to do so would be to engage with BDSM subcultures as they are, not as they are imagined to be. The principles of sexual citizenship, sexual rights, and rights to self-actualisation and flourishing through access to authentic sexual expression are compelling. And it is true that nurturing a sexually just contemporary culture should accommodate people's capacity to consensually express their full sexual selves without fear of sanction. More prosaically, accommodating this defence also helps to destigmatise non-normative sexual practices. That would be accompanied by closer engagement with what otherwise violent practices mean to the people who practice BDSM themselves. Greater awareness, de-stigmatising conversations about BDSM and enhanced knowledge about it would facilitate better and more effective engagements with BDSM when it enters the courtroom, not as spectacularised, but rather unboxed; evidenced (Sheff, 2021).

Pro-BDSM scholars have long elucidated the array of ways that BDSM is distinct from intimate partner violence or assault (Pitagora, 2013; Dunkley & Brotto, 2020). Scholars including Daniel Haley (2015), Monica Pa (2001) and Anne Onoma (2017), amongst many others, have outlined juridical pathways which might be adopted to facilitate this development. Risky practices such as breath play or knife play – both of which we have encountered in the cases analysed in this book – are popular. They are said to be thrilling, erotic, and to enhance sexual pleasure. Expert BDSM educators have warned that there is 'no way whatsoever' that breath play can be conducted without serious risk of cardiac arrest (Wiseman, 1997, p. 437). And yet, as research like that of Debby Herbernick et al. (2021) demonstrates, people are increasingly curious about breath play and want to give it a go. Merely prohibiting strangulation will not stem this curiosity. Rather, as BDSM educator Jay Wiseman also notes:

> There is a great deal of ignorance regarding what actually happens to a body when it's suffocated or strangled, and that the actual degree of risk associated with these practices is far greater than most people believe. I have noticed that, when people are educated regarding the severity and unpredictability of the risks, fewer and fewer choose to play in this area, and those who do continue tend to play less often. (1997, p. 440)

With better knowledge and less stigmatising discourse, people who are curious about BDSM can have better access to information about how to practice safely and with risk awareness; the distinction between BDSM and abuse will be better understood; victims of injury occurring during a BDSM or BDSM-adjacent encounter might feel more empowered to engage the criminal justice system if they want to.

We have seen how, in the USA, the introduction of 213.10 into the Model Penal Code (MPC) shows how a consent defence might be articulated. Of course, the version articulated in the MPC is one that is not expansive – consent must be 'explicit'– so it captures only some of how BDSM operates (Williams et al., 2013). In 1995, the Law Commission Report no. 139: Consent in the Criminal Law received significant numbers of submissions from different groups of BDSM practitioners including heterosexual and homosexual BDSM practitioners (named the Lives of the Secular Saints (1995, p. 134), one pro-BDSM action group called 'Countdown on Spanner' (Law Commission, 1995, p. 136), and the campaign group SM Gays (Law Commission, 1995, p. 140).

Together, these disparate voices detailed the social reality of BDSM practice; that it is sexually fulfilling, that it is an alternative sexual expression, that it comprises sexual activities beyond penetrative sex (Law Commission, 1995, p. 136); that it is conducted safely; that 'consent is everything'; that it is self-policing – 'an overly aggressive top does not get to top, because word gets around' – that it is built on trust, and so on (Law Commission, 1995, p. 138). The picture painted in these representations is nuanced, unspectacular, and comprises the voices of diverse practitioners of BDSM themselves. As an archival piece, it offers an invaluable insight into what can be said about BDSM and how little many of the principles espoused by respondents to the Commission paper have changed. The array of information submitted for consideration led the Commission to propose that 'the law ought not to prevent people from consenting to injuries caused for ... sexual purposes', subject to exceptions concerning the severity of injuries sustained. This, in the direct aftermath of the *Brown* decision, marks a significant shift in approach (or rather the potentiality of one).

And yet, it was noted in the Law Commission's Eighth Programme of Law Reform (2001) that the response to the 1995 proposals had been substantial, the analysis of the 'difficult legal and philosophical issues which it threw up [was] lengthy and painstaking' (Law Commission, 2001, p. 48). Responses were 'high polarised' and the complexity, density, and sensitivity of the issues at hand meant that the Law Commission declined to give any further commentary on whether there should be a defence of consent in sexual practices (Law Commission, 2001, p. 49). Through thoughtful engagement with the subtleties and specificities of BDSM practice, we came close to developing a pragmatic way to talk about non-normative sexual practice in England and Wales without giving the green light to practices which are an affront to human flourishing. The discourses in that report show us what is possible when difference is met with compassion and authentic intentions to understand difference. But the thorniness of the topic continued to undo this thinking. It continued to spectacularise it.

So, would creating a consent defence work? Possibly. But creating a consent defence would not be the end of the story. Even if a consent defence was available in all jurisdictions, even if the practices of sexual subcultures were to be better understood and less stigmatised in criminal justice settings, we still need to create worlds where rape myths have no logic, where rape culture is undone and where the structural violences of which the criminal justice system are a part are undermined.

As we see in the cases analysed here, even in contexts where judges' comments have been suffused with sex positive entreaties not to 'take a view' on, or moralise about, decisions that women who have been killed have made to get to this point (about casual sex, about sex work, about wandering about alone at night), these have been countered with rape myth accepting narratives which paint different pictures about women; ones that are less accommodating. We know that a consent defence will not be enough, because we see how consent discourses are also weaponised in cases like rape, *where it is a defence*. Yes, consent defences could have helped defendants in *Brown* exonerate themselves, but in all instances where a consent defence is available in the context of BDSM (in Germany, for instance, or Sweden, or under the MPC), that defence is available insofar as it does not 'cause or risks serious bodily injury' (MPC, 2013.10, p. 114) (is this easier to define than more than 'transient or trifling'?). In *Brown*, we have seen that even though none of the participants needed medical attention after their encounters, their injuries (lacerations, marks, cutting and bruising) were considered to be more than 'transient or trifling'. Indeed, maybe a transient injury takes a few hours to heal at most.

But, if, following the MPC for example, the threshold is that injury must not be serious, can we be sure that a consent defence would have been available? Evidence from the judgments in *Brown* show that judges were appalled by what took place. One 'victim' had a fishhook inserted into his penis; clearly this is an alarming image to the outsider. That the hook was sterilised and that any lacerations healed without medical intervention was mentioned but was sidelined. The decision to read as seriously injurious an act which was likely not to be is deliberate. It makes dangerous elements of sexual practice which are not. The alarm about BDSM sexual practice between men in the context of HIV/AIDS panics has been highlighted elsewhere (White, 2006). Would this risk of infections have been enough of a serious or perilous injury to be undone by a consent defence, had it been available?

The cases of *Lambda* and of *Pi* concern conscious, deliberate BDSM practice. What impact would something like MPC have on cases like these? In line with what the MPC recommends, some evidence of consent negotiation were evidenced in the contract in the case of *Lambda*, and in the online conversations about limits and safe words in the case of *Pi*. The contract gave Lambda 'free use' of Aye's body, which looks a lot like consensual non-consent (CNC). For a defence of consent to have been available to Lambda using something like the MPC, he would still have to evidence how safe words were communicated and limits were drawn within a CNC context. We know that Aye told Lambda that she could not take any more pain after her tattooing. He whipped her with a rope, regardless. For a defence of consent to have been available to Pi, who by Bee's account bruised and bit and penetrated her against her will, the negotiation of these acts being acceptable, or permitted, would have to be evidenced. Instead, we have her use of the safe word and violation of preset limits (which were evidenced by their Skype conversations and conversations about limits that Bee had had with her friends). A defence of consent would not have been available to Lambda or Pi following the guidance lain out in the MPC which allows for this defence.

Though the injuries that the women sustained were not serious or life-threatening (though they were potentially more than transient and trifling, and certainly were not what the women wanted or consented to), the fact that both defendants violate the boundaries set up prior to engaging in their BDSM practice, would vitiate the supposed consent of their partners. MPC-like guidance would have helped to protect, rather than undermine, the women's sexual autonomies. I make these observations even though, as we know, both Lambda and Pi were exonerated anyway. This conundrum is an expression of the troubles that grip contemporary sexual discourses. Sexual exceptionalism, sexual squeamishness, the way that these discourses vacillate between rejecting rape myths and making sense of the world through them are also expressions of this trouble.

BUILDING NEW WORLDS?

> the laws and the courts have a way of obliterating truth as women experience truth … our work is deeper; we must change not only what is legal and what is not legal, but what is acceptable (Russell & Griffin, 1977, p. 17)

I opened this chapter with the words of feminist activist Karen Rian. Her words come from her chapter critiquing sadomasochism. As is probably clear by now, I am not against sadomasochism (at least not in very much, and not in this book – see Fanghanel, 2019). A text like *Against Sadomasochism*, which does little to hide its perspective on BDSM, might seem an unlikely starting point for working a way through an impasse such as this. I have juxtaposed this opening with Califia's pro-BDSM unapologetic thirst for feminist freedom. Together they are unlikely bedfellows. However, here I want to draw attention to the commonalities which are built across these two positions: a call for gendered freedoms and a rejection of the socio-cultural which traps us all. As we also saw in Chapter 2, the positions that some commentators take about BDSM, harbour nuances that should encourage us to think. The rejection of sadomasochistic desire as innate (born this way) encourages us to think about the necessarily socio-cultural influences on how that desire is understood, articulated and engaged with. The rejection of anti-BDSM discourses as puritanical challenges the compulsory hypersexual qualities that those sceptical of sex positivity also avow (Lorde & Star, 1982). Recognising the neoliberalised way in which choice, responsibility and self-articulation are expressed in pro-BDSM discourses enables us to reconsider first, the commodification of sexual practices that we have come to accept, and second, the potentiality that communitarian, non-hierarchical, more cooperative approaches to sexuality might afford (Hein, 1982). This is not to do away with pro- or anti- sadomasochistic discourses, beyond questioning how helpful these dichotomies are for meaningful critical thought. It is to engage instead with what we can do with difference (Rian, 1982).

One of the reasons why creating a consent defence is both probably a good idea and yet not enough is because both positions slide around over a socio-cultural context which is patriarchal, which is heteronormative, which is ageist and ableist, and complicit in entrenching these lines of inequality. One way or the other, what they might do – their potentiality – is striated by the texture of this background. In their appeal for a sex positive approach to fostering social and legal change, Aimee Wodda and Vanessa R Panfil (2021) ask whether nuanced approaches to consent, sex which is wanted and that which is not wanted, and harm reduction are compatible with, or even possible within, existing criminal justice frameworks. Susan Griffin (1977), cited above, is also a contributor to the *Against Sadomasochism* tract, and whilst she was writing against pornography, she also identifies the same limitations that trouble Wodda and Panfil (2021). The criminal justice system may be an inadequate starting point for these transformations in sexual justice. The criminal justice system harbours the potentiality to enact violence in the way that it condemns, moralises, normalises, silences and excuses (it is beyond the scope of this book to demonstrate all the ways in which this happens, but suffice, perhaps, to point out that that this is cut along (at least) racialised, classed, sexualised, ableist lines). That it does this is also an expression of the context in which it operates. Rather than simply asking how criminal justice can be better, we would also do well to wonder how socio-cultural contexts might be better, beyond this. We have to change what is acceptable.

REACHING ACROSS DIFFERENCE

My appeal to the feminist scholarship that we encounter in Ruth Linden and her colleagues' (1982) text shines a small light on some of what might bring about this betterment. Binary oppositions between pro- and anti-sex work, pro- and anti-porn, pro- and anti- BDSM are, we have seen, more complex than first appears. Far more fruitful are encounters across difference which approach that difference with curiosity. The loving perception and world travelling that we encountered in Chapter 5 helps us here. Love, here, is not mere acceptance and erasure of difference. It is not a silencing of discord or debate. It is rather a commitment to foster understanding from different epistemological positions. For our purposes, it is not about saying that BDSM is emancipatory, or that female masochism is a myth, or that consent is always and already enough in the debates that we have engaged in. It is about doing the work to appreciate, make space for and seek to understand those differences.

The sex positivity that Wodda and Panfil (2021) demand, and that judges in many of the cases discussed here do proffer, would then be one that is not undermined by the familiar comfort of sex negativity that we have also seen. It could be underpinned by a world travelling which authentically accommodates sexual subcultures which are consensual even if we do not share them. An object lesson in YKINMKBYKIO, perhaps. Beyond sexual subcultures, an approach which seeks to understand difference and plurality fosters the potential to create richer, more nuanced, less spectacularised knowledge about those differences. To trouble those differences.

Because this troubling offers a turning point, *hope* becomes a generative force to propel this world travelling. Hope is offered by Rebecca Solnit (2016) as a pragmatic tool to employ in the face of difficult circumstances; in the face of crisis. Hope encourages us to imagine an alternative way of doing and being. It drives us to face down the manifest difficulties of building these alternatives. The Old English etymology of 'hope', hopa, means 'confidence in the future'. This not naïve hope that things will turn out OK. That sits on its hands and waits. It is the fire which ignites the passion for change; for *something else*. I said in Chapter 1 that we can trouble contemporary knowledge about sexuality. Failure – the failure of criminal justice perhaps – offers us a crucible with which to transform how we deal with sexuality. Hope becomes the fire with which that transformation is forged. By believing that there are different, other, better ways of encountering sexuality – especially sexuality in a criminal justice context – hope becomes an engine which drives us to open that black box and to despectacularise what it is we think that we know about sexual practice. But, more tangibly, what would this look like?

LEARNING BETTER FUTURES

As I began to point to in Chapter 5, creating and sharing better knowledge about non-normative sexuality is a start. Elisabeth Sheff (2021), D. J. Williams et al. (2013), and Dunkley and Brotto (2020), all point to the importance of education as a tool for creating better futures. We see some of how this has worked (and gone awry) in the context of BDSM and its interaction in the mainstream, as awareness of BDSM subculture has grown and various elements of its practice entered the mainstream (we saw some of this in the case of *Gaskell* (2018) and *Gamma* (2018), amongst others).

We have seen how these elements are rarified and spectacularised, but with better knowledge about BDSM subculture as it is understood by practitioners themselves (including, for instance, the fact that it *is* understood by BDSM practitioners themselves and not just something that happens by accident (Weinberg et al., 1984)), then the distinction between BDSM and abuse is easier to perceive. Jonathan Herring (2023) is perhaps rightly concerned that intimate partner violence and coercive control could be disguised as BDSM if a consent defence were available to defendants, but with better education about BDSM, this disguise would be harder to get away with. Cara R. Dunkley and Lotti A. Brotto (2020), Dulcinea Pitagora (2013) and Amy E. Bonomi et al. (2013) have all demonstrated how BDSM and abuse can be distinguished – including attending to abuse within a BDSM relationship – and the contributors to that 1995 Law Commission Report on consent are incredibly eloquent on the matter.

Better knowledge about the role of consent, its complexity and its limitations will also inform considerations of BDSM cases where women are there to give their account of events, and ones, where, as in the majority of the cases in this book, women have been killed. Where instead, attempts to construe their consent come from their backgrounds, vulnerabilities and promiscuities around otherwise impenetrable black holes. Here, I am talking about education for criminal justice professionals, for juries, for everyday citizens, even for children in schools. Sex positive education may help us here. Of course, we have seen how sex positivity itself can be spectacularised for sex negative ends, and how it can invite objections that it is apolitical. Transformative education which employs sex positive tactics will need to be wary. When educative approaches present non-normative sexual practices including sex work, BDSM or casual sex as neither good nor bad, this empowers those who engage with them, and those who do not, to encounter them at face value. That is, they may cause harm, they may not; they may be something I have always wanted to do, I may be doing it to make you happy; you may feel differently about it afterwards, you may not, but the acts themselves are not *a priori* good or bad. They only acquire meaning as good or bad, or anything, because of the socio-cultural context against which they take place. And understanding this, through education, helps us to see this background.

This neither-good-nor-bad approach brings me to my penultimate offering; one that posits a move against sexual exceptionalism.

FOSTERING DE-EXCEPTIONALISM

Michel Foucault (1988 [1977], p. 200) famously stated that 'there is no difference, in principle, between sticking one's fist into someone's face, or one's penis into someone's sex'. His position was that by desexualising rape and other sex crimes, the disciplinary regimes of sexuality could be undone. Sexuality would lose its capacity to exert social and biopower. Sex crimes would be crimes just like any other offence against the person.

Some feminist commentators, in response, have balked at the suggestion that sexual violence is simply a violence among other violences (Plaza, 1981; Woodhull, 1988; Bell, 1991). They argue that to do so erases first, the specifically gendered dynamics of rape and the specific violation that women who experience rape and other sexual violence feel (Henderson, 2007) and second, how rape is constructed by 'social sexing', or the 'social production' of the sexed body (Cahill, 2001, p. 145). Joseph Fischel, too, might disagree with the opinion that being punched in the face is the same as being raped. Sex, as we have already seen Fischel (2019, p. 28) posit, is 'special' for an array of reasons. Somewhat unsatisfyingly, sex is special because it is. It is different to non-sex because it is. Why is it? Fischel's list of suggestions is only unsatisfying because it cannot give us an answer, and to this extent, Fischel is right. We do not know why sex is special. We only feel that it is, or that it should be. Certainly, we know that taboos, interdictions and anxieties about who can have sex with whom, how, and when, are cross-cultural across time and space. Even if we cannot agree on why it is special, we kind of feel that it is.

But what if we were to return to Foucault's suggestion that sex is not different? That sexual violence is a violence like any other? De-exceptionalising sex might help us to see more clearly what is going on when crimes which have sexual elements take place. In the context of many of the cases analysed in this book, women have been killed by men during a sexual encounter. The sex is at the centre of the crime, and yet, the killing of the women (who are suffocated, strangled or cut) is not intrinsically about sex. It only acquires a sexual element to it because of the consensual sexual conduct that is also taking place. Had, for instance, India Chipchase been strangled by Edward Tenniswood outside of a sexual encounter, she would still be dead, and he would still have been charged with (and found guilty of) murder. Indeed, often, the crimes that men who kill are charged with are not sexual offences, but crimes of murder or manslaughter. The sex is considered to be consensual, so it is not an aggravating factor, but rather a descriptive one: what were these people doing when she was killed?

Instead, we have seen how the exceptionalisation of sex in these cases – sex as a fetish object, sex as a curiosity, sex as something about which we are squeamish – has led to detailed excavation of women's sexual histories or proclivities even though these have no material bearing on the way in which they were killed. Focus on sex work (*Bailey*, *Mu*), focus on having or not having sex toys (*Coates*, *Mu*), focus on promiscuity (*Morton*, *Gaskell*, *Pybus*, *Foster*), focus on interest in non-normative sex (*Mu*, *Tenniswood*, *Pybus*, *Broadhurst*) all feature in these cases. They murk accounts of what has led to the deaths of the women. When sex is de-exceptionalised, we can see more clearly what has happened and we can do that without folding back onto rape myths and victim blaming discourses that we have seen in each of the cases that are analysed in this book.

When sex is de-exceptionalised, even talking about sex which is non-normative is less logically coherent. Normative according to what? Such a shift opens up possibilities for making space for sex that undermines heteronormativity, and which accepts different ways to encounter the erotic as equally valid as others.

Sex can also harm. Sex crimes do happen. If sexual expression is so intrinsic to human dignity and emancipation, as many other pro-BDSM activists have suggested (Haley, 2015; Pa, 2001; Cowan, 2010), then sexual violations also become an affront to that dignity. Justice systems must be better equipped to deal with that. De-exceptionalising sex and how we talk about it makes it more possible to talk about sex without shame. When complainants are not shamed for what they have been through, for things they have done in the past, or for decisions that have or have not made, then interrogating what has happened in the case of sex crime, of murder with sexual elements, of BDSM when it goes wrong, is more possible. When sexual practice is not spectacularised, not exceptional, is not considered freaky, or weird, or gross, or sad, when it is just a difference amongst other differences, we can develop critical, meaningful approaches to it, especially when it goes wrong.

BECOMING DISENCHANTED

I suggested at the outset of this book, and I have reiterated this throughout, that when BDSM and BDSM-adjacent cases are heard in court, different elements of consent, BDSM and sex positivity are rehearsed and spectacularised. Contemporary ways in which non-normative sexual practices are dealt with in courts in England and Wales are deeply unsatisfactory. I have presented some examples here but there are many more instances where rape myths and the normalisation of rape culture have emerged to exonerate defendants and to responsibilise victims. Even when we see, from a carceral perspective, the 'right' outcome occur (Gaskell, who pleaded guilty to manslaughter; Bailey, who is imprisoned for the murder of Teeling and who is serving a minimum term of twenty-nine years for it), even when we see that consent claims do not always 'work' to mitigate the actions of perpetrators, that they are mobilised at all means that they are potent with this possibility. In the service of this possibility, women's sexual histories, mental health struggles, loneliness and substance use are deployed, to their denigration.

Spectacularisation obscures what is really going in these encounters. It creates reified, idealised versions of consent, BDSM and sex positivity. Black boxed, the spectacle hides the detail. It fosters enchantment that is uncritical and unquestioning about what we know about non-normative sex, how we know it and how we talk about it. Fostering critical distance, becoming – following Max Weber – disenchanted with consent-as-panacea-that-will-save-us-all; asking more questions about what we are being told is BDSM or BDSM-adjacent practice, is one way to pierce the spectacle.

I have suggested that critical curiosity fostered through hopefulness and world travelling, and through creating and sharing better knowledge about sexual practices – especially those with which we might be unfamiliar – are ways in which to become disenchanted. Adopting the queer and feminist epistemological praxes that I have pointed to in this book helps us to develop an understanding of sexual practice that is less heteronormative, less misogynistic, less imperialist, less ableist, less ageist, less static, less familiar, less sure of itself, too. It encourages us to ask questions: to point to black holes and black boxes; to critique the myriad ways that unwavering faith in consent as an illocutionary act makes us comfortable, and rape myths do, too.

When BDSM sexual practice is demystified, and all the ways in which consent is used to silence, confound and undermine *as well as to empower* are exposed, we can reach a turning point and imagine different worlds of sexual justice. Disenchanted, unspectacular, we can continue the work of nurturing sexual justice in criminal justice systems and the social world, beyond them.

Cases Cited

Commonwealth v. *Appleby*, 380 Mass. 296, 402 N.E.2d 1051 (1980)
Lawrence v. *Texas*, 539 U.S. 558 (2003)
People v. *Jovanovic*, 263 A.D.2d 182, 700 N.Y.S.2d 156 (1999)
People v. *Samuels*, 250 Cal. App. 2d 501 (1967)
R v. *Broadhurst (John Anthony)*, [2019] EWCA Crim 2026
R v. *Brown*, [1993] 2 All E.R. 75 (H.L.)
R v. *Donovan*, [1934] 2 KB 498
R v. *Emmett*, [1999] EWCA Crim 1710
R v. *J.A. 2011 SCC 28*, [2011] 2 S.C.R. 440
R v. *Pybus*, [2021] EWCA Crim 1787
R v. *Slingsby*, [1995] Crim. L.R. 570 (C.A.)
R v. *Welch*, [1995] 25 O.R. (3d) 665 (Can. Ont. C.A.)
R v. *Wilson*, [1996] 3 WLR 125
R v. *Wilson*, [1996] 2 Cr. App. R. 241 (C.A.)
R v. *Wilson (Alan)*, [1997] QB 47

Bibliography

American Law Institute. (2021). *Model Penal Code*. Philadelphia, PA: American Law Institute.

American Psychiatric Association. (1994). *Diagnostic and Statistical Manual of Mental Disorders* (4th ed.). Washington, DC: American Psychiatric Association.

American Psychiatric Association. (2013). *Diagnostic and Statistical Manual of Mental Disorders* (5th ed.). Arlington, VA: American Psychiatric Publishing.

Angel, K. (2021). *Tomorrow sex will be good again: Women and desire in the age of consent*. Verso Books.

Appleton, S. F. (2021). Sex-positive feminism's values in search of the law of pleasure. In D. Brake, M. Chamallas, & V. L. Williams (eds), *Oxford handbook of feminism and law in the United States* (pp. 94–111). Oxford University Press.

Arendt, H. (2003 [1970]). *On violence*. Penguin Books.

Ashford, C. (2010). Barebacking and the 'cult of violence': Queering the criminal law. *Journal of Criminal Law*, *74*(4), 339–57.

Austin, J. L. (1962). *How to do things with words*. Harvard University Press.

Barker, M. (2013). Consent is a grey area? A comparison of understandings of consent in *Fifty Shades of Grey* and on the BDSM blogosphere. *Sexualities*, *16*(8), 896–914.

Baudrillard, J. (1994 [1981]). *Simulacra and simulation*. University of Michigan Press.

Baudrillard, J. (2017 [1976]). *Symbolic exchange and death*. SAGE Publications.

Bauer, R. (2014). *Queer BDSM intimacies: Critical consent and pushing boundaries*. Springer.

Bauer, R. (2021). Queering consent: Negotiating critical consent in les-bi-trans-queer BDSM contexts. *Sexualities*, *24*(5–6), 767–83.

Beckmann, A. (2001). Deconstructing myths: The social construction of 'sadomasochism' versus 'subjugated knowledges' of practitioners of consensual 'SM'. *Journal of Criminal Justice and Popular Culture*, *8*(2), 66–95.

Bell, V. (1991). Beyond the 'thorny question': Feminism, Foucault and the desexualisation of rape. *International Journal of the Sociology of Law*, *19*(1), 83–100.

Bennett, T. (2021). A fine line between pleasure and pain: Would decriminalising BDSM permit nonconsensual abuse? *Liverpool Law Review*, *42*(2), 161–83.

Benson, L. S., Gilmore, K. C., Micks, E. A., McCoy, E., & Prager, S. W. (2019). Perceptions of anal intercourse among heterosexual women: A pilot qualitative study. *Sexual Medicine*, 7(2), 198–206.

Beres, M. (2010). Sexual miscommunication? Untangling assumptions about sexual communication between casual sex partners. *Culture, Health and Sexuality*, *12*(1), 1–14.

Bertin, G. (2025). Creating a safer world – the challenge of regulating online pornography. www.gov.uk/beis.

Bird, A. (2002). Illocutionary silencing. *Pacific Philosophical Quarterly*, *83*(1), 1–15.

Bonomi, A. E., Altenburger, L. E., & Walton, N. L. (2013). 'Double crap!' Abuse and harmed identity in *Fifty Shades of Grey*. *Journal of Women's Health*, 22(9), 733–44.

Bows, H., & Herring, J. (2020). Getting away with murder? A review of the 'rough sex defence'. *Journal of Criminal Law*, *84*(6), 525–38.

Bows, H., & Herring, J. (eds). (2023). *'Rough sex' and the criminal law: Global perspectives*. Emerald Publishing Limited.

Bracewell, L. N. (2021). *Why we lost the sex wars: Sexual freedom in the #MeToo era*. University of Minnesota Press.

Bradley, E. (2023). Reacting to rough sex: The unexpected toll of section 71 Domestic Abuse Act 2021. In H. Bows, & J. Herring (eds), *'Rough sex' and the criminal law: Global perspectives* (pp. 167–83). Emerald Publishing Limited.

Bridges, A. J., Wosnitzer, R., Scharrer, E., Sun, C., & Liberman, R. (2010). Aggression and sexual behavior in best-selling pornography videos: A content analysis update. *Violence Against Women*, *16*(10), 1065–85.

Brown, A., Barker, E. D., & Rahman, Q. (2020). A systematic scoping review of the prevalence, etiological, psychological, and interpersonal factors associated with BDSM. *Journal of Sex Research*, 57(6), 781–811.

Burch, R. L., & Salmon, C. (2019). The rough stuff: Understanding aggressive consensual sex. *Evolutionary Psychological Science*, 5(4), 383–93.

Busby, K. (2012). Every breath you take: Erotic asphyxiation, vengeful wives, and other enduring myths in spousal sexual assault prosecutions. *Canadian Journal of Women and the Law*, *24*(2), 328–58.

Cahill, A. J. (2001). *Rethinking rape*. Cornell University Press.

Califia, P. (1981[1980]). Feminism and sadomasochism. *Publix sec: The culture of radical sex* (2nd ed., pp. 168–80). Cleis Press.

Califia, P. (1988). *Macho sluts*. Alyson Books.

Centre for Women's Justice, End Violence Against Women coalition, Imkaan, & Rape Crisis England & Wales (2020). *The decriminalisation of rape: Why the justice system is failing rape survivors and what needs to change*. Centre for Women's Justice.

Cossman, B., Danielsen, D., Halley, J., & Higgins, T. (2003). Gender, sexuality, and power: Is feminist theory enough. *Columbia Journal of Gender and Law*, *12*(13), 601–37.

Cowan, S. (2010). The pain of pleasure: Consent and the criminalisation of sado-masochistic assaults. In J. Chalmers, F. Leverick, & L. Farmer (eds), *Essays in criminal law in honour of Sir Gerald Gordon* (pp. 126–40). Edinburgh University Press. https://www.jstor.org/stable/10.3366/j.ctt1r22cn.15.

Cowart, M. R. (2004). Understanding acts of consent: Using speech act theory to help resolve moral dilemmas and legal disputes. *Law and Philosophy*, *23*(5), 495–525.

Creighton, A. M. (2022). Umwelt, enchantment, and McDonaldization. *Chinese Semiotic Studies*, *18*(4), 653–79.

Debord, G. (2021 [1967]). *The society of the spectacle*. Unredacted Word.

DeLaney, T. (2023). Consenting to change: The new sexual assault provisions of the Model Penal Code. *University of Cincinnati Law Review*, *91*. https://uclawreview.org/2023/05/03/consenting-to-change-the-new-sexual-assault-provisions-of-the-model-penal-code/.

Dobson, A. S. (2011). Hetero-sexy representation by young women on MySpace: The politics of performing an 'objectified' self. *Outskirts: Feminisms along the Edge*, *25*.

Doherty, S. (2022). Fetish clubs are under attack from council using 'archaic' laws. vice.com. https://www.vice.com/en/article/klub-verboten-crossbreed-tower-hamlets-council/.

Downing, L. (2013). Safewording! Kinkphobia and gender normativity in *Fifty Shades of Grey*. *Psychology & Sexuality*, *4*(1), 92–102.

Drdová, L., & Saxonberg, S. (2020). Dilemmas of a subculture: An analysis of BDSM blogs about *Fifty Shades of Grey*. *Sexualities*, *23*(5–6), 987–1008.

Dunkley, C. R., & Brotto, L. A. (2020). The role of consent in the context of BDSM. *Sexual Abuse*, *32*(6), 657–78.

Edwards, S. (2015). The strangulation of female partners. *Criminal Law Review* (12), 949–66.

Edwards, S. S. (2017). Assault, strangulation and murder – challenging the sexual libido consent defence narrative. In A. Reed, M. Bohlander, N. Wake, & E. Smith (eds), *Consent: Domestic and comparative perspectives* (pp. 104–19). Routledge.

Edwards, S. S. (2020). Consent and the 'rough sex' defence in rape, murder, manslaughter and gross negligence. *Journal of Criminal Law*, *84*(4), 293–311.

Edwards, S. S. (2023). Sexualizing the killing of women: The rise of the 'rough sex' defence in Anglo-American jurisdictions. *International Annals of Criminology*, *61*(1), 1–25.

Fahs, B. (2014). 'Freedom to' and 'freedom from': A new vision for sex-positive politics. *Sexualities*, *17*(3), 267–90.

Fanghanel, A. (2019). *Disrupting rape culture: Public space, sexuality and revolt*. Bristol University Press.

Fanghanel, A. (2020). Asking for it: BDSM sexual practice and the trouble of consent. *Sexualities*, *23*(3), 269–86.

Fanghanel, A., & Lim, J. (2017). Of 'sluts' and 'arseholes': Antagonistic desire and the production of sexual vigilance. *Feminist Criminology*, *12*(4), 341–60.

Fischel, J. J. (2019). *Screw consent: A better politics of sexual justice*. University of California Press.

Foucault, M. (1982). The subject and power. *Critical Inquiry*, *8*(4), 777–95.

Foucault, M. (1988 [1977]). *La folie encirclée* (Change Collective, 1977), reprinted in L. Krtitzman (Ed.), *Politics, philosophy, culture: Interviews and other writings, 1977–1984*. Routledge.

Foucault, M. (1998 [1976]) *The history of sexuality, Part one: The will to knowledge*. Penguin.

France, M. (1984). Sadomasochism and feminism. *Feminist Review*, *16*(1), 35–42.

Franke, K. M. (2001). Theorizing yes: An essay on feminism, law, and desire. *Columbia Law Review*, *101*, 181–208.

Galilee-Belfer, M. (2020). BDSM, kink, and consent: What the law can learn from consent-driven communities. *Arizona Law Review*, *62*, 507.

Garnier, M., & Harman, H. (2019). Men are using the narrative of women's sexual enjoyment to get away with murder, literally. *Huffington Post*.

https://www.huffingtonpost.co.uk/entry/rough-sex-murder-harriet-harman_uk_5d309e09e4b020cd9940533c.

Gavey, N. (2024). Deconstructing 'rough sex' in a New Zealand murder trial: Beyond the modern mythology of everyday kink. *Social and Legal Studies*. https://doi.org/10.1177/09646639241292689.

Gelder, K., & Thornton, S. (1997). *The subcultures reader*. Routledge.

Giles, M. (1994). R v Brown: Consensual harm and the public interest. *Modern Law Review*, *57*(1), 101–11.

Glick, E. (2000). Sex positive: Feminism, queer theory, and the politics of transgression. *Feminist Review*, *64*(1), 19–45.

Glickman, C. (2000). The language of sex positivity. *Electronic Journal of Human Sexuality*, *3*, 1–5.

Gotell, L. (2012). Governing heterosexuality through specific consent: Interrogating the governmental effects of R. v JA. *Canadian Journal of Women and the Law*, *24*(2), 359–88.

Green, J. E. (2005). Two meanings of disenchantment: Sociological condition vs. philosophical act – reassessing Max Weber's thesis of the disenchantment of the world. *Philosophy and Theology*, *17*(1/2), 51–84.

Halberstam, J. (2011) *The queer art of failure*. Duke University Press.

Haley, D. (2015). Bound by law: A roadmap for the practical legalization of BDSM. *Cardozo Journal of Law and Gender*, *21*, 631–56.

Hanna, C. (2001). Sex is not a sport: Consent and violence in criminal law. *Boston College Law Review*, *42*, 239–90.

Harris, E. (1982). Sadomasochism: A personal experience. In R. R. Linden, D. R. Pagano, D. E. H. Russell, & S. L. Star (eds), *Against sadomasochism: A radical feminist analysis* (pp. 93–5). Frog in the Well.

Hebdige, D. (1979) *Subculture: The Meaning Of Style*. Methuen.

Hein, H. (1982). Sadomasochism and the liberal tradition. In R. R. Linden, D. R. Pagano, D. E. H. Russell, and S. L. Star (eds), *Against sadomasochism: A radical feminist analysis* (pp. 83–90). Frog in the Well.

Henderson, H. (2007). Feminism, Foucault, and rape: A theory and politics of rape prevention. *Berkeley Journal of Gender Law and Justice*, *22*, 225.

Herbernick, D., Fu, T. C., Valdivia, D. S., Patterson, C., Gonzalez, Y. R., Guerra-Reyes, L., & Rosenberg, M. (2021). What is rough sex, who does it, and who likes it? Findings from a probability sample of US undergraduate students. *Archives of Sexual Behavior*, *50*, 1183–95.

Herbernick, D., Guerra-Reyes, L., Patterson, C., Rosenstock Gonzalez, Y. R., Wagner, C., & Zounlome, N. (2022). 'It was scary, but then it was kind of exciting': Young women's experiences with choking during sex. *Archives of Sexual Behavior*, *51*(2), 1103–23.

Herring, J. (2023). Coercive control and rough sex. In H. Bows, & J. Herring (Eds.), *'Rough sex' and the criminal law: global perspectives* (pp. 31–51). Emerald Publishing Limited.

Hickman, S. E., & Muehlenhard, C. L. (1999). 'By the semi-mystical appearance of a condom': How young women and men communicate sexual consent in heterosexual situations. *Journal of Sex Research*, *36*(3), 258–72.

Hoople, T. (1996). Conflicting visions: SM, feminism, and the law. A problem of representation. *Canadian Journal of Law and Society/La Revue Canadienne Droit et Société*, *11*(1), 177–220.

Hopkins, P. D. (1994). Rethinking sadomasochism: Feminism, interpretation, and simulation. *Hypatia*, 9(1), 116–41.

Houlihan, A. (2011). When 'no' means 'yes' and 'yes means harm: HIV risk, consent and sadomasochism case law. *Law and Sexuality: A Review of Lesbian, Gay, Bisexual & Transgender Legal Issues*, *20*, 31.

Hurd, H. M. (1996). The moral magic of consent. *Legal Theory*, *2*(2), 121–46.

Ivanski, C., & Kohut, T. (2017). Exploring definitions of sex positivity through thematic analysis. *Canadian Journal of Human Sexuality*, *26*(3), 216–25.

Jenkins, R. (2000). Disenchantment, enchantment and re-enchantment: Max Weber at the millennium. *Max Weber Studies*, 11–32.

Jozifkova, E. (2013). Consensual sadomasochistic sex (BDSM): The roots, the risks, and the distinctions between BDSM and violence. *Current Psychiatry Reports*, *15*(9), 392–400.

Kaplan, M. (2014). Sex-positive law. *New York University Law Review*, *89*, 89–164.

Khan, U. (2014). *Vicarious kinks: S/M in the socio-legal imaginary*. University of Toronto Press.

Khan, U. (2016a). Hot for kink, bothered by the law: BDSM and the right to autonomy. Canadian Bar Studies Association. https://www.cba-alberta.org/Publications-Resources/Resources/Law-Matters/Law-Matters-Summer-2016-Issue/Hot-for-Kink,-Bothered-by-the-Law-BDSM-and-the-Rig.

Khan, U. (2016b). Take my breath away: Competing contexts between domestic violence, kink and the criminal justice system. In R. v. JA. *Oñati Socio-Legal Series*, *6*(6).

Khan, U. (2020). Kinky identity and practice in relation to the law. In C. Ashford, & A. Caine (eds). *Research handbook on gender, sexuality and the law* (pp. 362–78). Edward Elgar Publishing.

Kitzinger, C., & Frith, H. (1999). Just say no? The use of conversation analysis in developing a feminist perspective on sexual refusal. *Discourse and Society*, *10*(3), 293–316.

Krafft-Ebing, R. (2011 [1894]). *Psychopathia sexualis: The classic study of deviant sex*. Skyhorse Publishing Inc.

Latour, B. (1987). *Science in action: How to follow scientists and engineers through society*. Cambridge University Press.

Law Commission. (1994). Law Commission, Consent and Offences Against the Law (Law. Com. no. 134, 1994).

Law Commission. (1995). *Consent and the Criminal Law* (Consultation Paper no. 139). The Stationery Office.

Law Commission. (2001). The Law Commission Eight Programme of Law Reform (Law Com. 275). The Stationery Office.

Lee, E. M., Klement, K. R., & Sagarin, B. J. (2015). Double hanging during consensual sexual asphyxia: A response to Roma, Pazzelli, Pompili, Girardi, and Ferracuti (2013). *Archives of Sexual Behavior*, *44*(7), 1751–3.

Levi-Strauss, C. (1955). The structural study of myth. *Journal of American Folklore*, *68*(270), 428–44.

Linden, R. R., Pagano, D. R., Russell, D. E. H., & Star, S. L. (eds). (1982) *Against sadomasochism: A radical feminist analysis*. Frog in the Well.

Lorde, A., & Star, S. L. (1982). An interview with Audre Lorde. In R. R. Linden, D. R. Pagano, D. E. H. Russell, & S. L. Star (eds), *Against sadomasochism: A radical feminist analysis* (pp. 66–72). Frog in the Well.

Lugones, M. (1987). Playfulness, 'world'-travelling, and loving perception. *Hypatia*, *2*(2), 3–19.

Mackenzie, F. (2023). The rough sex defence in the UK. In H. Bows, & J. Herring (eds), *'Rough sex' and the criminal law: Global perspectives* (pp. 151–65). Emerald Publishing Limited.

Meredith, J. (1982). A response to Samois. In R. R. Linden, D. R. Pagano, D. E. H. Russell, & S. L. Star (eds), *Against sadomasochism: A radical feminist analysis* (pp. 96–9). Frog in the Well.

Miller, D. J., & McBain, K. A. (2022). The content of contemporary, mainstream pornography: A literature review of content analytic studies. *American Journal of Sexuality Education*, *17*(2), 219–56.

Milne, E. (2021). *Criminal justice responses to maternal filicide: Judging the failed mother*. Emerald Publishing Limited.

Ministry of Justice. (21 February 2023). *Government crackdown on image-based abuse*. https://www.gov.uk/government/news/government-crackdown-on-image-based-abuse.

Moran, L. J. (2017 [1995]). Violence and the law: The case of sado-masochism. Reprinted in L. J. Moran (Ed.), *Sexuality and identity* (pp. 249–75). Routledge.

Moser, C. (2019). DSM-5, paraphilias, and the paraphilic disorders: Confusion reigns. *Archives of Sexual Behavior*, *48*(3), 681–9.

Moser, C., & Madeson, J. J. (1998). *Bound to be free: The SM experience*. Continuum International Publishing Group.

Muehlenhard, C. L., & Hollabaugh, L. C. (1988). Do women sometimes say no when they mean yes? The prevalence and correlates of women's token resistance to sex. *Journal of Personality and Social Psychology*, *54*(5), 872.

Mullender, R. (1993). Sado-masochism, criminal law and adjudicative method: R v. Brown in the House of Lords. *Northern Ireland Legal Quarterly*, *44*, 380.

Newmahr, S. (2011). *Playing on the edge: Sadomasochism, risk, and intimacy*. Indiana University Press.

Nussbaum, M. C. (2011). *Creating capabilities: The human development approach*. Harvard University Press.

O'Byrne, R., Hansen, S., & Rapley, M. (2008). If a girl doesn't say 'no' … Young men, rape and claims of 'insufficient knowledge'. *Journal of Community and Applied Social Psychology*, *18*(3), 168–93.

O'Higgins, J., & Foucault, M. (1982). II. Sexual choice, sexual act: An interview with Michel Foucault. *Salmagundi* (58/59), 10–24.

Onoma, A. (2017). Legal censure of unconventional expressions of love and sexuality; finding a place in the law for BDSM. *Hastings Women's Law Journal*, *28*, 25.

Ormerod, D. (1994) Consent and Offences against the Person Law Commission Consultation Paper no. 134. *Modern Law Review*, 57(6), 1994928-942.

Pa, M. (2001) Beyond the pleasure principle: The criminalization of consensual sadomasochistic sex. *Texas Journal of Women and the Law*, *11*(1), 51–92.

Paris, J., & Ault, M. (2004). Subcultures and political resistance. *Peace Review*, *16*(4), 403–7.

Pascoe, J. (2024). The Whiteness of Consent. In L. James-Hawkins, & R. Ryan-Flood (eds), *Consent: Gender, power, and subjectivity* (pp. 11–23). Routledge.

Pitagora, D. (2013). Consent vs. coercion: BDSM interactions highlight a fine but immutable line. *New School Psychology Bulletin*, *10*(1), 27–36.

Plant, B. (2007). Playing games/playing us: Foucault on sadomasochism. *Philosophy and Social Criticism*, *33*(5), 531–61.

Plaza, M. (1981). Our damages and their compensation: Rape: The will not to know of Michel Foucault. *Feminist Issues*, *1*(2), 25–35.

Rian, K. (1982). Sadomasochism and the social construction of desire. In R. R. Linden, D. R. Pagano, D. E. H. Russell, & S. L. Star (eds), *Against sadomasochism: A radical feminist analysis* (pp. 45–51). Frog in the Well.

Richters, J., De Visser, R. O., Rissel, C. E., Grulich, A. E., & Smith, A. M. (2008). Demographic and psychosocial features of participants in bondage and discipline, 'sadomasochism' or dominance and submission (BDSM): Data from a national survey. *Journal of Sexual Medicine*, *5*(7), 1660–8.

Ridinger, R. B. (2006). Negotiating limits: The legal status of SM in the United States. In P. J. Kleinplatz, & C. Moser *Sadomasochism* (pp. 189–216).

Ritzer, G. (1996). The McDonaldization thesis: Is expansion inevitable? *International Sociology*, *11*(3), 291–308.

Robinson, P. H., & Dubber, M. D. (2007). The American Model Penal Code: A brief overview. *New Criminal Law Review*, *10*(3), 319–41.

Roma, P., Pazzelli, F., Pompili, M., Girardi, P., & Ferracuti, S. (2013). Shibari: Double hanging during consensual sexual asphyxia. *Archives of Sexual Behavior*, *42*, 895–900.

Rothman, J. E. (2012). Sex exceptionalism in intellectual property. *Stanford Law and Policy Review*, *23*, 119.

Rubin, G. S. (2002 [1984]). Thinking sex: Notes for a radical theory of the politics of sexuality. In R. Parker, & P. Aggleton (eds), *Culture, society and sexuality* (ch. 9). Routledge.

Russell, D. E. H., & Griffin, S. (1977). On pornography: Two feminist perspectives. *Chrysalis*, *1*(4), 11–17.

Sagarin, B. J., Lee, E. M., & Klement, K. R. (2015). Sadomasochism without sex? Exploring the parallels between BDSM and extreme rituals. *Journal of Positive Sexuality*, *1*(3), 50–5.

Sentencing Council. (n.d.) a. *Sexual Assault: Offences outline*. https://www.sentencingcouncil.org.uk/outlines/assault/.

Sentencing Council. (n.d.) b. *Assault: Offences outline*. https://www.sentencingcouncil.org.uk/outlines/assault/.

Sheff, E. (2021). Kinky sex gone wrong: Legal prosecutions concerning consent, age play, and death via BDSM. *Archives of Sexual Behavior*, *50*(3), 761–71.

Sherry, P. (2009). Disenchantment, re-enchantment, and enchantment. *Modern Theology*, *25*(3), 369–86.

Singy, P. (2012). How to be a pervert: A modest philosophical critique of the Diagnostic and Statistical Manual of Mental Disorders. *Revista de Estudios Sociales* (43), 139–50.

Solnit, R. (2016). *Hope in the dark: The untold history of people power*. Canongate Books.

Sowersby, C. J., Erskine-Shaw, M., & Willmott, D. (2022). Masochist or murderer? A discourse analytic study exploring social constructions of sexually violent male perpetrators, female victims-survivors and the rough sex defense on Twitter. *Frontiers in Psychology*, *13*, 867991. https://doi.org/10.3389/fpsyg.2022.867991.

Srinivasan, A. (2021). *The right to sex*. Bloomsbury Publishing.

Stiles, B. L., & Clark, R. E. (2011). BDSM: A subcultural analysis of sacrifices and delights. *Deviant Behavior*, *32*(2), 158–89.

Stychin, C. F. (1995). *Law's desire: Sexuality and the limits of justice*. Routledge.

Stychin, C. F. (2001). Sexual citizenship in the European Union. *Citizenship Studies*, *5*(3), 285–301.

Sundén, J. (2023). Digital kink obscurity: A sexual politics beyond visibility and comprehension. *Sexualities*, *27*(8). https://doi.org/10.1177/13634607221124401.

Swift, J. (2021). Toxic positivity? Rethinking respectability, revaluing pleasure. *South Atlantic Quarterly*, *120*(3), 591–608.

Tannen, D. (1991) *You just don't understand: Women and men in conversation*. Virago.

Thomas, E. J., Stelzl, M., & Lafrance, M. N. (2017). Faking to finish: Women's accounts of feigning sexual pleasure to end unwanted sex. *Sexualities*, *20*(3), 281–301.

Townsend, L. (1983). *The leatherman's handbook II*. Carlyle Communications Limited.

Træen, B., Fischer, N., & Kvalem, I. L. (2021). Sexual variety in Norwegian men and women of different sexual orientations and ages. *Journal of Sex Research*, *59*(2), 238–47. https://doi.org/10.1080/00224499.2021.1952156.

Tsaros, A. (2013). Consensual non-consent: Comparing EL James's *Fifty Shades of Grey* and Pauline Réage's *Story of O*. *Sexualities*, *16*(8), 864–79.

Van Ouytsel, J., Punyanunt-Carter, N. M., Walrave, M., & Ponnet, K. (2020). Sexting within young adults' dating and romantic relationships. *Current Opinion in Psychology*, *36*, 55–9.

Vance, C. (Ed.) (1984). *Pleasure and danger: Exploring female sexuality*. Routledge and Kegan Paul.

Vance, C. S. (1993). More danger, more pleasure: A decade after the Barnard sexuality conference. *New York Law School Law Review*, *38*, 289.

Vera-Gray, F., McGlynn, C., Kureshi, I., & Butterby, K. (2021). Sexual violence as a sexual script in mainstream online pornography. *British Journal of Criminology*, *61*(5), 1243–60.

Vogels, E. A., & O'Sullivan, L. F. (2019). The relationship among online sexually explicit material exposure to, desire for, and participation in rough sex. *Archives of Sexual Behavior*, *48*(2), 653–65.

Walling-Wefelmeyer, R., & O'Neill, T. (2021). 'There are a lot of bad dominants, mostly men, where it's basically abuse dressed up as a kink': Victim-survivors' everyday navigation of BDSM, kink and fetish. *Child and Family Law Quarterly*, *33*(4), 363–78.

Weeks, J. (1998). The sexual citizen. *Theory, Culture and Society*, *15*(3–4), 35–52.

Weeks, J. (2002). *Sexuality and its discontents: Meanings, myths, and modern sexualities*. Routledge.

Weinberg, M. S., Williams, C. J., & Moser, C. (1984). The social constituents of sadomasochism. *Social Problems*, *31*(4), 379–89.

Weiss, M. D. (2006). Mainstreaming kink: The politics of BDSM representation in US popular media. *Journal of Homosexuality*, *50*(2–3):103–32.

Weiss, M. (2009). Rumsfeld!: Consensual BDSM and 'sadomasochistic' torture at Abu Ghraib (ch. 10, pp. 180–201). In E. Lewin & W. L. Leap (eds), *Out in public: Reinventing lesbian/gay anthropology in a globalizing world*. Blackwell.

Weiss, M. (2011). *Techniques of pleasure: BDSM and the circuits of sexuality*. Duke University Press.

White, C. (2006). The Spanner trials and the changing law on sadomasochism in the UK. In P. J. Kleinplatz, & C. Moser (eds), *Sadomasochism: Powerful pleasures* (pp. 167–87). Routledge.

Wilkinson, E. (2009). Perverting visual pleasure: Representing sadomasochism. *Sexualities*, *12*(2), 181–98.

Wilkinson, E. (2011). 'Extreme pornography' and the contested spaces of virtual citizenship. *Social and Cultural Geography*, *12*(5), 493–508.

Williams, D. J., Prior, E., & Wegner, J. (2013). Resolving social problems associated with sexuality: Can a 'sex-positive' approach help? *Social Work*, *58*(3), 273–6.

Williams, D. J., Thomas, J. N., Prior, E. E., & Christensen, M. C. (2014). From 'SSC' and 'RACK' to the '4Cs': Introducing a new framework for negotiating BDSM participation. *Electronic Journal of Human Sexuality*, *17*(5), 1–10.

Wiseman, J. (1997). *SM 101: A realistic introduction* (2nd ed.). Greenery Press.

Wodda, A., & Panfil, V. (2020). *Sex-positive criminology*. Routledge.

Wodda, A., & Panfil, V. R. (2021). Sex-positive criminology: Possibilities for legal and social change. *Sociology Compass*, *15*(11), 11–25.

Woodhull, W. (1988). Sexuality, power, and the question of rape. In I. Diamond, & L. Quinby (eds), *Feminism and Foucault: Reflections on resistance* (pp. 167–76). Northeastern University Press.

Yardley, E. (2021). The killing of women in 'sex games gone wrong': An analysis of femicides in Great Britain 2000–2018. *Violence Against Women*, 27(11), 1840–61.

Index

EU Authorised Representative:
Easy Access System Europe Mustamäe tee 50, 10621 Tallinn, Estonia
gpsr.requests@easproject.com

Printed and bound by CPI Group (UK) Ltd, Croydon, CR0 4YY
14/09/2026
02216782-0001